The Lightbringer Unbridled

Ravenwolf

D1595640

First Paperback Edition: March 2021

ISBN: 978-1-63848-788-3 (print)
ISBN: 978-1-63848-790-6 (ebook)

Hyperbole Publishing
www.houseofravenwolf.com

Stories of Hope, Love & Empowerment

5

Trust the Magic of New Beginnings

I may not have always ended up where I
wanted to go,
But I've always arrived exactly where I was
meant to be.
All the broken roads and wishes that didn't
come true nearly broke me sometimes.
I never understood why so many doors closed
and why I faced so many dead ends.
My happily ever afters seemed to always turn
into goodbyes and my heart broke countless
times into heartache.
It's hard to keep hoping when every single
time, your hopes and dreams keep getting
crushed along the way.
I never got what I thought I deserved ...
Not because I didn't deserve what I wanted,
but because I was worth so much more.
I started being okay with settling and stopped
reaching for the stars.
Everyone will tell you the same cliches "it'll be
okay" and "it'll work out," but you start
wondering who it really works out for.
Tears welled in my eyes so often as I just
wanted to be happy.

I didn't have the answers – in fact, I didn't even have the questions any more.

I had stopped listening to my heart and started listening to my doubts.

I lost my self-worth and began to believe I wasn't good enough anymore.

Yet, for all the people in my life that surrounded me with love, I was utterly alone.

That's the thing about losing your way – you don't know where to start back.

When you finally understand the irony of life – It takes sadness to appreciate happiness, heartache to understand love … it takes darkness to find your way back to the light.

There's days when I stumble and fall, losing the hope that keeps me going.

It's hard to believe when you have all the reasons to give up.

But this is a new year and a new chance.

My journey will be a tale of triumph, but it will also be a story of failures and mistakes.

I've learned not to be defined by my bad choices, and I discovered a way to never lose hope in myself or my path.

I can't go back and rewrite the old chapters, and truth is, I wouldn't want to if I could.

Those are the times that made me who I am,
that forged my fire in the flames of struggle.
I've never met a strong person with an easy
past, and I'm no exception.
So, these are the moments that invigorate my
soul and fill my spirit ...
The times when I close my eyes, breathe in
deeply and reclaim my courage when it falters.
This is the time ...
When I trust in the magic of new beginnings.

Be the Love You Never Received but Always Wanted

I know what it feels like to want to be loved so much it hurts ...

The emptiness that aches in places that you can't explain.

I've been the person trying so hard to love someone that didn't love me back the way I deserved.

I know how it feels to be left holding the pieces of your broken heart because you gave someone everything and they said it wasn't good enough.

I've been the person who's done all the things right to make a relationship work, put in the effort only to see the other person just give up.

I've tried to save others who wouldn't be saved or partners who couldn't accept me for who I was ...

Instead, who tried to change me into their version of what they thought they wanted.

Maybe they loved my attention and adoration, maybe they loved the idea of being in love or were just scared of being alone.

Truthfully, I can't tell you why it never worked out before because I've always loved hard when there was love to be had and given my all to those I thought I loved.

I used to think it was because that I wasn't good enough or that I was doing something wrong, but I know now it was because they didn't deserve me.

So, take my hand in yours and come to me, honestly and openly.

I can't promise I'll be perfect or never make mistakes, or that every day will be great ... because none of that is real.

But I'm here, standing in front of you, asking you to love me bravely and loyally.

And you can always know one thing:

I'll always be there for you … I'll be the love you've always wanted but never received.

I'll love you with every last bit of my heart, mind and soul … each and every day.

Meet me halfway and let's go find the stars.

Dreams are better when you share them with someone you love.

Someday You Will Look Back and Know Exactly Why It Had to Happen

I sit here in the dark, fighting back the tears while I'm lost in the thoughts and memories of what we once had.

The pain … it can hurt so much that it makes all else seem not to matter.

How can something you wanted so much not work out the way you'd always hoped?

I loved you with all my heart, gave our relationship everything, but still, I'm alone and trying to hold it together … and failing.

Tears flow down my cheeks as the images of us cascade across my mind …

Memories of what we had makes me smile … and cry.

Yes, there were amazing moments, but there were also angry fights and hurtful words.

There's so much I wish I could take back and change, but we can't undo the damage that's been done.

I try to tell myself that we will still work out, that we will find a way, but deep down, I know this is goodbye.

I don't know where we went wrong or exactly why we fell apart, because there was so much love there –

But sometimes, love just isn't enough.

Things started slipping through my fingers as we grew apart and every disagreement caused our hearts to become a little more bitter.

I close my eyes and I just try to stop the thoughts, the memories, the pain … but I can't. Everything is too fresh and too real.

I never knew emotional pain could feel so physical and so intense, until now.

It's in these moments, at our lowest, that we approach the crossroads.

I was standing there, in my overwhelming grief, not knowing what to do or how I would make it through this ...

When a bleep from my phone drew my attention.

I wiped my eyes and tried to see through my tear-stained vision.

Words from one of my oldest and dearest friends.

"If it wasn't meant to be, nothing you can do will change that … don't spend so long staring at a lost past that you forget how to embrace a beautiful future of possibility ..."

I smiled and shook my head at those wise words.

Sometimes, when you're at your lowest, you will see a sign … it was up to me to take it to heart.

But she was so right … I was so focused on the why of what happened that I would never make peace with it until I let it go.

I had to accept it so my heart could begin to heal.

I may never know the why or how, only that it did.

I'd never see the new doors opening if I kept staring at the closed door of us.

I closed my eyes, inhaled deeply and made myself a promise I would remind myself of every single day.

What's meant to be will always find a way, and my future and happiness is all in my hands.

If it's meant to be, it's up to me.

I'm letting go of the past to make room for what may be ...

I don't know what tomorrow will bring, but I know for reasons I can't explain,

That someday, I will look back and know exactly why it had to happen ... and I will smile, Because my broken road led me right to where I always needed to be.

The Only Happiness You Are in Control of Is Your Own

I learned a long time ago that my life and my path was mine to control.
The choices I made and my mindset would always be what forged my future.
I still had challenging days and trying times, but I realized how I reacted to those troubles would define who I was.
I always wanted a life full of sunshine and rainbows, and while there will always be some darkness and rain mixed in ...
I knew I could rise above them.
Sure, it wouldn't always be pretty, I'd stumble and fall more often than not, but I would never stay down.
Somehow, I'd dig deep and find my resolve to keep pushing forward.
I always remembered who I was and what I deserved and never settled for anything less.
No matter how I failed or how often I cried, down and out, I always found my voice again.
I'd take back my magic and rekindle my fire and climb back on the path to where I was meant to be.

I never dwelled on the trying times and I always looked for the sunlight.
I noticed the beauty all around me and reveled in the gorgeous moments that would someday become wonderful memories.
I'd make a point to enjoy the laughter of small children and smile at their innocent spirit.
I'd soak in the beauty of nature and its magnificence in all things great and small.
I'd marvel at a radiant sunrise and love the dying hues of a somber sunset.
I would, no matter how hard, try to fall in love with being alive every day.
Come what may, through life's triumphs and tragedies, my happiness was always mine to own ...
And that's just what I'll do for the rest of my life.
Be happy, be in the moment and always ...
be thankful for each and every day that I'm alive.

Even on the Grueling Days My Eyes Are Still Full of Stars

There are always going to be hard days, I always knew that.
Times when life brings me to my knees and threatens to unravel everything I've worked so hard to build ...
When my days are full of struggle and my nights marked by unrest.
When I can't see the light because the darkness is closing around me, and I don't know which way to turn.
The sleepless nights and tears for no reason sometimes weigh me down and make my spirit weary in a way that sleep cannot remedy.
I always knew I'd never have all the answers, but the days that I don't have any answers at all bring me to my wit's end.
Tears of frustration stream down my face as I struggle to find my way during those storms of discontent ...
And the truth is,
There are moments that I don't know if I can keep going.

You see, it took me being so far down that I feared being lost forever to understand how to rise again from the abyss of despair,
Where the shackles of angst weighed me down so powerfully that I didn't know if I would survive ...
But it was in those moments that I found myself and uncovered my truths that had escaped me for so long.
They say you have to experience sadness to appreciate being happy ...
Well, the same is true for being at your lowest … that's how you see the top again.
I had a choice to make ... either give up or fight back.
It's not easy and there are days when I just want to quit … but I know that I'm better than that.
I've never been a quitter, now is no different – I'm never going to let the light go out from my eyes ...
See, that's when I faced the fire and rose again stronger than before, forged from the flames that could have consumed me.
It was the hardest thing I've ever had to do, but I realize now that I can do more than survive ...

I can thrive.

I'm turning my wounds into wisdom and remembering my courage.

Nothing can ever take away who I am and what I'm meant to be.

Maybe I'm a little broken, but I'm beautiful.

Maybe I'm a little hard, but I'm loving.

Maybe I'm a little tough, but I'm soft inside.

There may be darkness around me sometimes ... But that will only make it easier to see the stars that will forever be in my eyes.

Here and Where You Are

No matter where I am or the day I've had,
My heart and soul are always with you.
Miles apart or beside each other,
I'm always there, holding your heart.

We found each other against impossible odds,
Worlds apart and a chance somehow found,
You've given my heart a home,
And my soul a companion for always.

The very moment we lose ourselves in
embrace,
Time slows and the world dissipates
As we seek refuge in our hidden place,
Our cocoon of surreal love and peace.

You've had me since the very first moment
When our eyes met and souls collided,
And I knew in that instant,
I'd finally found my forever in you.

I know that we've had our ups and downs,
Tragedies and triumphs will always be,
But together, we can weather any storm,

And our love will always see us through.

So, as our days carry us to places apart,
Know that I will carry your love with me,
Tucked away in the safety of my heart,
And forever will you be ...
Beautiful in my eyes.

Patience, Protection … Loving and Living Their Dreams

She needs more than the normal woman, for she's been down the wrong road too many times, and her heart has been broken more often than not.

She's yearned for love her entire life but found all the wrong men that were never what she needed.

She wanted incapable men to be something they could never be, and they disappointed her without fail.

Truthfully, she knew better than to get her hopes up, but that hopelessly romantic side of her wouldn't let her stop believing that she would find true love.

She did her best to stay positive, keep hoping alive and believing that the right one was just around the corner.

She knew what she wanted and even knew what it should feel like, but always ended up holding the pieces of a shattered heart.

Men often didn't know what to think of her, for she wasn't the type to tiptoe and keep to herself – just the opposite, most of the time.

They'd call her loud, say she had an attitude or claim that she was too much to handle.
She realized that the men that said those things were just too weak for her ...
She needed a strong man with a passionate soul, one that could engage her mind and capture her heart.
She craved a deeper soul love that many were just incapable of experiencing.
After all, baring yourself to another person could be truly frightening and some are not able to appreciate that level of honesty.
She waited for the one who could see her soul for its true depth and beauty, unafraid to connect with her in the most visceral and authentic way imaginable.
She knew the right man wouldn't tell her all the things she wasn't or couldn't be, he'd adore her depths, unravel her mysteries and treat her heart with patience and care.
She'd finally be able to forget all the frogs she'd kissed along the way because she'd have found her fairy tale ...
And though she knew it'd still have its challenges, she'd have someone to stand beside her through the storms.

She'd always tried to tell herself that what she wanted was very simple, though in the most complex way possible.

All her life, she'd been holding out for her happily ever after, and she was just fine taking her time, no longer trying to make lesser men into what she wanted them to be ...

It wasn't fair to her or to them.

She would wait for the love that was meant to be, one that she knew she would recognize the instant it found her ...

Soul deep, passionate and genuine, she wouldn't have to force, twist or convince anything or anyone ...

Especially herself.

This time, she was done holding out for a hero, She didn't care about accepting just any man or any love.

She would love her life, enjoy her moments and chase the stars until he showed up ...

Then, she'd just keep going, with him right beside her,

Loving and living their dreams,

Just the way it was always meant to be.

I Would Rather Die from Passion Than Live Feeling Nothing at All

I want out of the boxes, the labels and definition of what I should be.
I won't accept average, ordinary or lackluster when it comes to my life … I want more.
No, I need more.
I crave the passion of a life full of adventure where I will never have regret.
I'm going to do the things everyone has always dreamed of doing and then keep going.
I yearn for the allure of the open road, enjoying beautiful sunsets and lying under bright star-filled skies.
But more than that, I want to experience all the things that will fill my soul and electrify my spirit.
If I can't put my heart into, then I will take myself out of it.
I deserve to know the beauty of passionate love, and I will taste the danger of living exciting dreams.
It's not enough for me to just have hopes and desires ...

I will find wonder in the ordinary moments and seek fulfillment in the best that life has to offer.
I refuse to sit back and let things happen to me ... No, I'm owning my experiences and taking charge of my life.
My happiness is my responsibility, and I intend to relentlessly pursue the mysteries and adventures that make me feel alive.
I know every day won't be thrilling and there will still be bad days, but it doesn't mean I have to linger in those moments.
No, I choose to live outside the box, chase my dreams and see the beauty all around me.
If I can dream it, I can be it.
If I can think it, I can become it.
There are no second chances and what ifs that I'll ever be okay with.
So, maybe I won't change the world or be famous, but I don't want to be.
I want to fall in love with being alive every day, knowing that I lie my head down at night having given it my all.
I don't care what the world thinks about who I am or what I want, I'm an original old soul who loves hard, lives fully and doesn't look back

except to smile at the wonderful moments of a life well lived.

So, take my hand, let's turn our faces to the sun, lose ourselves in adventure and go make some amazing memories.

Me, you and forever ...

What do you say?

I Tried So Hard to Fix You I Didn't Notice That You Were Breaking Me

I never wanted us to fall apart the way we did … but then, no one ever does.

Our love was strong, powerful and passionate … the sort of love that we all search for our entire lives.

But as we found that our attraction was intensely overwhelming sometimes, we overlooked a lot of other things ...

Things we should have been paying attention to.

We may have seen the truth but refused to acknowledge it, I can't really say.

I tried to do whatever I could to make you happy ...

Somewhere along the way, I began trying to fix you, to do whatever I could to make your life better … or so I thought.

I poured so much of myself into you and us that it slowly began to eat at me ...

Tearing me apart, little by little.

I don't know why I thought I had to save you, that you needed my help to fix your problems … But that's just who I am, I guess … a fixer.

I tried to do for you so much that I stopped doing for myself.

I lifted you up when you wouldn't even stand on your own … and it broke me a little more every time.

So, now we stand at a crossroads, and I don't know where the path leads from here.

We have the love that most only dream of, but that's been lost a little as we fought to keep going forward.

I don't have any answers other than that I know I love you and I'll do whatever I can to make this work.

I've fallen to my knees, drained as the struggle of carrying us both threatened to tear me apart … But I'm rising again and finally remembering my own strength,

A little more every day, a little braver each time.

I know now I can't save you or fix you – only you can do what needs to be done to make yourself happy.

So, as I stand in front of you, hand outstretched, the choice is yours to make.

Is our love worth fighting for, or does this chapter close our story?

I know we will do what's best for both of us,
just always know that I did all I could for love,
for us.
If I have to walk away, I'll do it knowing I gave it
my all.
In the end, that's all we can really do ...
Live, laugh and love 'til we can't anymore.
I believe in you, in me, in us ...
I know we can emerge from this battle
stronger, wiser and closer.
What's meant to be will always find a way, as
will we.
Through the storms, I know we can make it,
together ...
Now more than ever, I truly believe.

Sometimes It's Best to Simply Appreciate the Time You Had Together and Move On

As I turned and watched you walk away, I fought the tears back as the memories of us flashed through my mind.

The good times and the bad, the joy and the pain, the love and the laughter … I saw it all. It made me sad and happy at the same time, and my heart felt like it could explode.

I now know that sometimes, you have to cherish the good memories and let the bad stuff go ...

I want to remember us and smile, because all the bad things won't do me any good to keep reliving ...

So, I'm banishing those bad moments and thoughts because I don't need them anymore ... and I'm going to hang onto the bits of happiness we once had,

Not the sadness that our pain will bring back.

I don't know how we got to this place, where we lost our way from the love that was once so amazing.

We celebrated the good times and stood together during the hard days, but in the end, what we had just wasn't meant to be.

I'll always love you and you'll forever have a place in my heart, but as they say, sometimes love just isn't enough.

We could never communicate through the hardships the way we both wanted to – almost as if we spoke different languages at times.

You'd wall yourself off from me and we just couldn't talk – maybe you just didn't want to.

I did my fair share of things wrong, too, I know that now.

We can't go back and change the way things happened, undo the fights and hurt feelings, and I know now it's for the best.

It hurts in a way that I've never felt, but that's how you know you really care about someone ... I wish sometimes, I could just turn off my heart ...

But I can't.

I won't.

We made the best of a passionate love that was never meant to be, and we hung on for too long to a story that was always going to end.

We loved, we fought, we tried and we failed ...

But we never stopped loving, no matter how hard it got.

So, as you disappear from my sight, tears stream down my face for the memories we made together.

I can't imagine my life without you, but now, I'll have to do just that.

I'll probably bawl when I hear our favorite song and sigh when something reminds me of you, but life will be different now, and I just have to accept that.

Maybe we will meet again someday and things will be different, but I won't let myself think about that.

For now, I'm going to smile about the memories, laugh about the joy we had and celebrate a love that once was ...

My days will be strange without you in them, but this is the road I must take now.

I'm going to rediscover myself and what makes me happy.

This is my time to dig deep and find my joy in all the places I stopped looking because of us.

I owe that to myself, and more than that, I owe it to my heart and my future.

I don't have the answers, and I may never figure them all out, but all I can do is very simple ...
Keep my face to the sunlight and live in the moments of my life.
That, for now, will have to be enough.
One day at a time, I'll find my way back to where I'm meant to be, I know that now ...
I'll find the happiness I once lost along the way to my dreams.
I just didn't know where to look before ...
Sometimes, the most beautiful joys can come out of the worst things if you know how to let go of the pain ...
This time, I'm going to open my heart, free my mind and forever seek the light.

I Choose Both

I know there are going to be days when you just can't get it together, because I have them too.

When you're running late, wearing mismatched socks and forgot to eat as you're bounding off to your day, and that's just life sometimes.

I don't expect you to be perfect because I'm far from it.

In fact, what makes us perfect for each other is how wonderfully all our jagged edges fit together.

There will be days you need my strength and other times when I'll need your positivity, but that's what will carry us through the hard times.

Things won't always go as planned, but as long as we can depend on each other, we will find our way through.

I've celebrated your victories on your best days and I've held your hand during the hard times ... I've seen your best and your worst, and I choose both, for always.

I'll have my moods and you'll have your days too, but if we stick together and remember what's important,

There's nothing we can't do together.
True love isn't about just being happy during the easy times and good days, it's about standing strong through all the days, both good and bad.
It won't always be easy, in fact it may be rocky sometimes, but so long as we have love in our hearts and hope in our spirits –
You, me and us –
We will always be better together than apart,
And we always will be,
This I promise you.

Every Time I Follow My Heart It Leads Me to You

I've spent a lot of my life making wishes on stars,
Hoping that love would find me sooner rather than later.
I've gone down a lot of broken roads and tried to make partners out of projects,
And all of those relationships ended in heartache … until I met you.
You were everything I never knew I needed until you showed me how amazing love could be.
You loved me at my worst and celebrated me at my best, holding my heart and hand through it all.
Our love did more than fulfill me, it made me want to be a better person – for me, for you, and for us.
You're my refuge from any storm and my happy place at the end of a day,
For you've shown me what love can truly be.
So, every time I smile when your name pops up on my phone, it's because you've changed my heart, my love and most of all, my life.

Every day, in every way ... when I'm greeted by your beautiful face,
I can't help but fall head over heels for you all over again ...
After all, isn't that what a real love story is all about?
Falling in love is at the heart of every happily ever after ...
That's just what I plan to do, with you, for the rest of our lives together ...
Fall in love all over again, every day,
Now and for always.

I'm Not Holding Out for a Hero

I don't need someone to come along and try to
be what I don't need.
Save the fixing, completing and saving for
somebody else, I'm not holding out for a hero
... I'm waiting for the one who wants to be by
my side for life's beautiful adventures.
I'm whole and fulfilled just the way I want, so
my soulmate doesn't have to make me happy
... I do that all on my own.
I want that person who laughs at my bad jokes,
kisses me in the rain and holds my hand
through the storms.
Not just anyone, but that once in a lifetime
partner who is weird in all the same ways I am.
The person who I can have a conversation with
across a room in a single glance,
the one who I can't wait to embrace at the end
of each day and the love that always be true.
I want the soulmate that masters the big stuff
but gets the little things right, too.
Dances in the kitchen, impromptu road trips
and random kisses just because they feel like
it.

Sure, I want the same things everyone else wants: love, respect, equality and courtesy ...
But I deserve so much more:
Deep soul love that never ends, long meaningful conversations about life, even passionate attraction that starts with my heart and mind.
So, I guess it's just a matter of finding that one person who loves like I do:
Passionately, deeply and faithfully ...
The partner who nurtures my soul, engages my mind and encourages my dreams.
I know what I'm seeking may seem impossible, but I know what I'm worth and what I deserve ... And I believe they're out there looking for me too.
I'll never settle, make do or accept anything less than what I know I need.
I know I'm a handful, even a mess sometimes, but I'm all the best kinds of beautiful disaster and depth that yearns to be loved.
My story will be filled with ups and downs, triumphs and tragedies, but most of all, it will be full of wonderful soul love and glorious passionate adventure ...
And I wouldn't have it any other way.

How Do You Sleep When Your Heart Is at War with Your Mind?

I try to do whatever I can to quiet my thoughts, but often, nothing works.

The television, music … anything I can find to drown out the deafening noise of my mind.

I tell myself that everything will work out the way it's supposed to, but my heart won't rest, and my thoughts never quit.

I replay where I've been and what's happened, the turns and twists of our relationship, and still, I lie there and stare at the ceiling ...

Consumed by the relentless overthinking that is my way.

I can't remember a time when I could turn off my mind, and I've come to accept that's just who I am ...

But when my heart battles my mind at night, it can become almost overwhelming.

My head tells me to let it go, make peace with the broken road I've traveled, but my heart won't let me.

It tells me to keep fighting, to hold on, that loving someone means struggling and making it through the hard times together.

I can't help but cry in these times when everything inside me is at war with what I should do.

The tears flow as I fight to regain my composure, but it's impossible sometimes to keep it together.

Maybe when I get up tomorrow I'll feel better or have some ideas about what I should do, but right now, I just feel utterly lost.

Conflict wages inside every corner of me, with no end in sight.

I just want … peace.

I close my eyes and think back to simpler times when love was new and hope was fresh.

I find myself slowly drifting off as those warm thoughts wrap around me like a comforting blanket, giving me much-needed peace.

As my heart and mind slow, my dreams whisk me away to a more serene place and my last thought before succumbing to exhaustion is but a simple wish ...

Maybe tomorrow, somehow, I'll find my way to a happier place … and there,

I'll remember what it means to be content again ... where my mind and heart can finally agree with what's best for me.

Until then, I'll just do what I can with what I have ...

And the simple reminder that gives me solace if but for a moment as I drift off:

It's always darkest before dawn.

I know that tomorrow will have to be a better day ...

If not, I'll just keep pushing forward and hope for moments of quiet midst my thoughts.

For me, for now, that will have to be enough.

Consumed by Silence Instead of Forgiveness

It'll never be what she says that you should pay
the closest attention to, but rather the things
that stay in her mouth and heart … the words
that she does not say.
The love of a woman is a powerful and
beautiful thing, but her silence can be truly
deafening.
Hear what she says, soak in her voice and take
heart in the things she shares,
But if you want to truly begin to understand the
complexity and depth of a woman, pay close
attention to all the things she doesn't say.
Her eyes will speak countless words that her
soul yearns to express, yet she never does.
Her quiet resolve and the strong facade that
she maintains for the world to see protect her
in ways that mere words never can.
The walls around her heart, the hidden beauty
of her soul, the latent dreams and unspoken
desires are all part of her mystery.
Cherish her, appreciate her and respect her,
for she fights battles that you'll never know or
understand.

She'll tuck it all behind few words ...
"I'm okay" … "everything's fine" …
Those are the painful whispers of an internal
war that she wages so very often.
You'll rarely see her tears, for she often cries in
solitude – the shower, the car, in bed.
She doesn't want the world to judge her or for
others to worry, she just has those moments
when her heart erupts tears of release, and
she needs that momentary meltdown to keep
going.
So, don't ever mistake her silence for lack of
concern, for it's just the opposite.
She has a million things to tell you, but often
just doesn't even know where to start.
Be patient, be respectful and be
compassionate.
And whatever you do, don't push her over the
edge too far, or she might never come back the
same way you once knew ...
Because when she has made her decision,
there's no more chances and no more starting
over ...
There's just silence.
She has no more words, no more tears and
nothing left for you, for your relationship ...

She won't talk any more about what's
happened or what you can do, because it won't
matter.
She's done.
She's silent because she has nothing left for
you ...
She's walking away.
It's that same silence that will tell you – if you
know how to listen –
Everything you ever wanted to know about the
real beauty and depth of a woman ...
Just don't wait too long and lose the wonderful
opportunity to love her in all the ways she truly
deserves ...
Before it's too late ...
Because when it is,
All you'll hear is her silence.

Pain Shapes a Woman into a Warrior

Truthfully, she didn't choose her life or her
path,
It chose her.
She didn't have any other options and she did
the only thing she knew:
Survive.
She fought and clawed her way back from the
edge so many times, she almost fell ...
Into the darkness,
Into despair,
Into not thinking she could ever dig her way out
of the pain.
Broken hearted and almost numb to the world,
she bowed her head and closed her eyes.
No, she didn't have the answers – in fact, there
so many questions she had, instead.
How would she survive?
How could she come back from the
brokenness?
Would she ever be the same?
It was in that moment that she realized that she
didn't want to be the same ...
She wanted to be better.
She knew she could be more.

She needed to be stronger.

Where once a woman had fallen to her knees now rose a warrior in her place.

She stopped worrying and started living.

Her pain didn't vanish, but she stopped wallowing in it.

What she had been through would never define her,

But how she rose again would become who she was.

She had been lost for so long, depending on the wrong men to make her happy, and she always ended up holding the pieces of her shattered heart.

In fact, she had all but forgotten who she was because she had looked to them to define her existence.

No more would she seek happiness in another person –

This was a journey that was long overdue ...

The struggle to find her joy wouldn't be an easy one, she knew that, but she realized that loving herself first would be the way she would make her way back home to who she was always meant to be.

She had been knocked down in her desire to be loved, and her broken soul now realized that she needed more than the love of a man ... She desperately longed to love herself.

Rising to her feet, tears staining her face, she mustered a painful smile.

She knew what she had to do, even if she didn't know how – she understood why.

She wasn't just a survivor; she was a warrior ... And this time, she was done chasing fools and playing games.

She would kindle the fires of her courage from the pain of her past ...

And it would do what nothing else could:

Make her stronger, better and wiser.

A warrior now stood where a failed woman had once fallen ...

Beautiful, proud and free.

I Felt Your Love as Plainly as the Sun

When you found me, I thought I knew love.
I believed I understood what love meant,
How it really felt and how it was to go ...
How wrong I was in all those thoughts.

You showed me feelings that I had never
known,
In ways I'd never imagined,
In truths I couldn't have understood,
When you gave me your heart.

The contentment in your arms,
The fire in your desire,
The love in your eyes
The ferocity of your passion ...
All beautiful parts of you that I'll always
treasure.

Those feelings were just the door creaking
open
To a cascading flood of the wonders of you,
That your heart, your love and your soul
Showed me from the very first time we
touched.

You didn't just make me feel loved,
You helped me learn how to love myself,
Held my hand through the struggles,
And wiped away my tears during the pain.

I'll never know how I came to be so blessed
when I found you,
Only that I drift off every night and wake each
morn,
With a happiness in my soul that you brought
to me,
A light in my heart that beats stronger for you.

Come what may, no matter where life leads us,
I'll walk the path with you by my side,
Thankful, hopeful and blissful,
As plainly as the sun's warmth above,
Loving you, for the rest of our lives.

Wild and Free

She was the free spirit that lived without the need of anyone's permission or acceptance. She had always been all the things no one ever understood, and she was okay with that. An old soul, empathetic and wild, she made no excuses for who she was and how she lived. She lived in the moments of her life, reveling in the beauty all around her and losing herself in the wonders that she beheld.

She believed deeply in the things most people had forgotten or overlooked: passionate love, soul depth and fiery desire.

Her life was almost perfect, it seemed ...

Until she met him.

He showed her how to be more than just wild, but how to spread her wings and truly fly.

His love and appreciation for all the things that she cherished most about herself empowered her in such a way that she found a newfound courage in the possibilities that she had once avoided.

It was one thing to be wild, yet another to be free.

Their love elevated her wild beauty to a level she had never known, and she loved him fiercely for who she was with him.

He was everything she never knew she needed but now craved intensely ...

Respect, empowerment ... the click they felt was unlike anything she'd ever known.

He just got her in a way no one else ever had. From across a room or even miles away, he just had an uncanny way of sensing her energy and being there for her – sometimes, when she didn't even know she needed him to be.

She had never looked for a man to complete her, but when his love took hold of her heart, she found everything about herself and her life became that much better.

Most of the time, she couldn't explain how he had enriched her life, only that their love was something long ago written in the stars,

A destiny that she knew was always meant to be.

No matter how high she flew or the challenges that faced her, she now attacked her life with a fiery spirit that would not be denied ... the fears from the past just seemed to melt away.

Before she met him, she was always wild,
strong and beautiful ...
Now, she was so much more than that ...
He had helped her see the way to be
something greater and stronger ...
Now, she was finally free.

The Idea vs. the Reality of Me

I know you thought you were in love with me,
but we've both now realized that there's a big
difference between fantasy and reality.
All the wishes and desire in the world can't
make two people fall deeply in love if it's not
real.
And as much as that tears my heart into
pieces, we can't ignore the truth.
We both wanted this to be the fairy tale, but it's
something very different ...
You loved the idea of me and what I
represented, but the reality of who I am wasn't
something you were prepared for.
You said I was too much or a handful, but I'm
just me ... no more and no less.
I'm real, I'm authentic and I'm always going to
speak my mind.
I don't believe in taking a back seat or being
silenced.
Love is about equality, respect and the
courage to love someone unconditionally ...
And that's an ideal you're not ready to embrace
yet.

I'll never fault you for not knowing exactly what you wanted, but I'm not going to accept your reality of what I should be.

I'm bold, I'm beautiful and I'm unique in the ways that matter to me.

Sure, I'm a mess some days and a complete disaster on others, but I always own who I am and my shortcomings ...

But I'm more than just what I'm not.

I'm strong, I'm vibrant and I know what I want, who I am and what I deserve.

Truthfully, you realize now what you need in a partner, because I'll never be that person,

And that's okay.

So, I don't harbor any bad feelings as we go our separate ways, and I will always wish you the best.

We tried to love each other but sometimes, love just isn't enough.

We fought for what we thought we wanted, and in the end, we knew what we had wasn't the fairy tale we had hoped for.

I'll always care about you and hope you find what you're looking for,

But I'm glad we discovered our truth before we hurt each other worse in the process.

So, as I walk away, know that I'll think of you from time to time and I'll smile.

That's what I'll remember about us, the good times and happiness.

Next time, I'll love even harder when there's love to be had.

Thank you for loving me in your way and letting me go like you did.

You'll always be special.

May you always find the sunlight in your days and peace in your nights ...

Perhaps in the next life we will meet again, and things will be different.

Until then, I'll just be chasing my dreams,
Strong, wild and free.

If They Can't See Me Shine, It's Because They're Looking for the Person I Used to Be

I'm done playing it safe and abiding by the rules.
I've waited far too long to let my heart and soul shine.
I've been cooped up, kept down and repressed for so long, I almost forgot who I was.
That ends now.
I'm taking back my power and unleashing all of my beautiful vibrance.
I'm not going to let anyone tell me what I can and can't do anymore, because this is my life and my chance to shine brightly ...
I refuse to hide who I am anymore or dull my sparkle because other people can't handle me.
They can step up or step aside: this is finally my time to fly high.
The world tried to make me believe that I was less than I am and thought I would be okay with being ordinary.
I'm done listening to the naysayers and the negativity,

Because I've got one chance to live my life the way I choose, with no regrets, and I'm seizing that opportunity now.

I'm not starting a new chapter; I'm throwing the old book away and rewriting a new story altogether.

Forget the labels, the definitions and the permission of society to tell me what's acceptable and okay,

I'm just don't care anymore.

No one has walked my path and they weren't there for my struggles,

So why should I let anyone tell me how to shine?

More than that, I've found my wings, broken out of my cage and I'm remembering all those forgotten dreams that once inspired me.

Maybe I won't change the world or do everything I want, but that doesn't mean I won't be all that I can,

Chase my dreams with relentless optimism and reach for the stars every day.

So, I've found my voice and seen my chance to become the best I can be ...

Starting with today, no more apologies, excuses or settling.

My day, my way, on my terms.
Win or lose, rise or fall, rain or shine, I'll either
go down in flames or rise again like the fire ...
The most beautiful part of it all ...
Is that it's all up to me.

The Broken Girls Have the Deepest Love

She knows she's not like the others, she can't just move on from heartbreak.
Her walls are higher than theirs because she's different in how deeply and fiercely she loves.
She's not passive, soft or weak in the love she gives.
You'll never mistake her heart for a candle in the wind, she's a roaring wildfire.
Her love is something most men can't handle – deep, soulful and passionate, she's the person who pours her everything into her love ...
Which is why she suffers so much when her heart is broken,
Why it utterly devastates her depths when love's hope dwindles away.
She'd rather tackle her life with reckless abandon and fierce passion than to just survive.
If she gave all of herself into love and still she failed, she'd do it all over again – as often as she could.
She wasn't afraid of being hurt in search of

love … she feared never giving love everything ... To waste her life never having lived, loved and pursued the desires of her heart fearlessly. She knew there was no reward without risk, and to her, love would always be the greatest reward and feeling there ever was.

She'd rather be burned alive by the fire of her passionate love than to wither away in the loveless void of never having loved at all.

Truthfully, the others would say she was broken in the most desperate way possible, but that's just because they didn't understand her … And they didn't have to.

She was quite content with who she was and her choices, for she lived without apologies or regrets.

What they called broken, she knew was beautiful instead.

All the little cracks of the pain she had faced had created the beauty of who she was ...

For that was how the light got in.

Her old soul was deep and yearned for the fire of love that she longed to find ...

But she never sacrificed who she was to make anyone else happy ...

She knew, deep down in places that she didn't

speak of, that her impassioned love was a rare and beautiful thing ...

She'd always guard her heart fiercely behind the walls that protected her, but she wasn't afraid to risk it all to chase the love she knew she deserved.

Yes, she was broken, she was beautiful and most of all,

She was free to choose her own path.

She'd throw herself into the fires time and again to find her true love ...

Regardless of the outcome, which was often heartbreak.

That's just who she was, and she owned it –

Every flaw, imperfection and failure.

But that's why she was what the others would never be:

Broken, beautiful, strong ...

And always free to pursue the fires of her heart.

The Smoky Fire of My Rebirth

I know now that I had to fall to my knees to rise
from my failures even stronger.
I am not defined by my struggles nor am I
limited by what I've done wrong.
No, those times that I fell and didn't know if I
could get back up – those were the lessons I
couldn't have learned any other way.
I stumbled, I fell, I cried and I hurt ...
But it was in the fires of my pain that I forged
the courage to pick myself up and rediscover
my power.
There're days when I don't feel like I can make
it, when a smile is almost impossible, and I
don't know how I'm going to get out of bed ...
But I find a way; I dig deeply and force myself
to keep going.
Maybe it's not pretty and perhaps I don't look
absolutely gorgeous on those days, but I'm
okay with that.
I'm always going to be beautiful in my own way
with as much style and charm that I can
muster.

The world thought I was at the end of my rope and that I wouldn't last any longer, and once, they might have been right.

Now, however, I've faced the fires of my failures and emerged a warrior made of the flames that once threatened to tear me apart.

I'm not afraid anymore … I've survived the worst that life could throw at me, and I'm still standing.

More than that, I found my voice and my hope. Darkness could never extinguish my light and I'm on my way to being alive in a way that is better than I've ever been.

I'll still have bad days and I'll still get knocked down, but I've realized that I don't have to stay down … I'm more than a survivor.

I'm a fighter … I'm a believer … I'm a dreamer. I have the bravery to fight for my dreams and the belief that I can achieve anything.

Forget all those people who thought I'd never make it and I'd give up.

That's not who I am.

I had to die in the flames to be reborn a passionate Phoenix capable of setting my heart on fire.

Where I've been has made me who I am … I'll never forget my anguish, for that is the fuel that empowers me to push harder and fight stronger.

So, as the smoke settles from the wreckage of my life that was, I stand amongst the ashes of my former self …

And from the midst of the burning embers of my trials by fire emerges a new me –

Capable of anything I choose, who believes that anything is possible and won't let anything or anyone stop me.

I'm done living day-to-day and minute-to-minute.

This is my chance, and my time is now.

Come what may, I've come alive in a way that electrifies my senses and inflames my soul.

So, bring me the storms and the fury,

I can handle it all.

Some people fear the fire.

I chose to become it.

I've turned my wounds into wisdom and my setbacks into a comeback.

Now it's time to watch me rise and shine …

Just like the fiery light I am.

That Cozy Kind of Love

She was a girl much like any other, except when it came to love.

Matters of the heart were something she didn't take lightly, and she knew exactly what she wanted ...

Only she couldn't sometimes put it into words. She knew she'd recognize the feeling of true love when it found her, because she'd encountered all the wrong kinds of love in all the wrong ways.

Those few that were "almost" the one and even the dead ends taught her all the things she didn't want in love ...

But verbalizing exactly what she wanted was almost impossible ...

She could tell you all the things she wanted in love and a partner,

But the intangibles – chemistry, goals, love languages ... that impossibly long and sometimes unknown list was hard to describe, because she hadn't found it all yet ...

Hence why she was still looking ...

Deep down in her heart she knew that when true love finally came knocking on her door,

she'd recognize it instantly.
She wanted the butterflies during kisses, the calm contentment in the embrace, the fiery passion of desire … she craved all of it,
And she wouldn't settle for anything less.
She knew what she deserved and was prepared to hold out for that dream.
Nothing worth having comes easy she realized, especially love.
So, while she was tired of kissing frogs looking for a prince, she wasn't ever going to be anyone's just another option.
She knew that love would come unexpectedly in its own time, and she was okay with that.
She knew that forever didn't happen on a schedule, and she spent her time and energy on being the best version of herself that she could be.
So, until love came calling, she would be chasing her dreams, enjoying her life and shining bright like the light she was,
Now and for always.

It's Never Too Late … You Just Have to Be Brave Enough to Choose

I'm done caring about what everyone thinks about my life and what I should do.
I'm not going to let fear keep me from doing what I've always wanted to do – chase my dreams.
Sure, I've made excuses and told myself all the reasons why I couldn't do something, but I was just lying to myself.
I was too afraid of failing, of what others might think or of stepping outside my comfort zone.
No more.
I lost my voice and my passion somewhere along the way, and it's time to reclaim everything them,
Piece by piece.
I know my journey won't happen overnight and it won't be easy, but I'm not going to rest until I start living my purpose.
I've let the "what ifs" rule my life for too long and it's left my soul empty and my spirit listless.
So, I'm done with simply existing or surviving my days,

I'm making a choice today to start a new chapter with a fresh beginning.

I'm taking back my power, turning my setbacks into a comeback and not letting other people or fear keep me from evolving into the best me that I can be.

Dreams don't have deadlines, and I know that changing my life is a process, but it's all up to me and the choices I make.

So, I'm going to stop listening to all the people who hold me back and I'm going to break out of the boxes and definition of what I "should be."

Truthfully, I know I'll be afraid of failure and not knowing what the next steps will be ...

But the beautiful thing about life is that I don't have to understand all the answers, just own my experience, and I'll never give up.

Courage isn't the absence of fear, it's just that pushing forward is more important ...

So, I'm closing the chapters on the me that I used to be, and I'm opening the pages to the person I should have become a long time ago.

My happiness matters more than the opinions of others or following the crowd.

I know I'm going to fall, stumble and hit rock bottom before I truly find my wings and learn how to fly.

And that's ok.

I choose all the things that I never could before:

I choose passion to fill my soul.

I choose happiness to fill my heart.

I choose courage to follow my dreams.

I'll rise, I'll fall and I'll turn broken chances into new opportunities ...

But most of all,

I'll be listening to my heart and living with my purpose.

My legacy will be many things, but they'll never say I didn't have the fire to forge a new beginning.

And the most beautiful part of all is that ...

It starts today, with me.

Even When Someone Won't Be in the Next Chapter … the Story Must Go On

As I turned and walked away, I felt the tears welling up in my eyes.
The memories of what we had and the love we once shared flashed through my mind in a long-since gone montage of happiness.
It's easy to remember the good stuff when you're thinking about someone –
My soul couldn't take reliving the heartache and pain that we had endured as a couple.
The bitterness and angst that made me cry so many nights … I simply didn't want to feel that again.
I looked back over my shoulder one last time at you, seeing you standing there, motionless as I walked away.
I could see your pain, eyes watering, and it hurt me deeply – maybe one of the hardest things I've ever had to do was walk away from you.
It was something that I had to do for us both to find happiness again.
We both knew that we couldn't make us work, no matter how hard we tried or how much we loved.

Sometimes, love just isn't enough.

You travel down a broken road so long with someone that sometimes you forget what you're fighting for anymore.

The why and the love gets replaced by trying to find a middle ground ...

You stop seeing the joy and beauty of your love and just try not to suffocate under the weight of anguish.

And that's never going to be enough for me – and it shouldn't be enough for you, either.

I smiled one last time as I turned a corner and saw you for the last time.

Those powerful moments can be overwhelming, but they're also a lesson of growth ...

Time slows to almost a standstill as your eyes meet for one last time ...

And then, it's like they were never there – such an important part of your life ... vanished.

We weren't ever meant to be and continuing to hold onto a broken relationship was making us both miserable.

In the end, saying goodbye to you and to us was one the hardest things I've ever had to do, but I know it's for the best.

I'll always love and care about you, that will never change.

Some people were meant to be in your heart, not your life.

So, as I close the chapter of our life and love, a solitary tear rolls down my cheek.

I'll never forget what you meant to me and the times we shared.

I'm making the hard decision to walk away to find real and lasting love ...

Most of all, for myself ... I had lost that part of me for so long with you.

Now, I'm taking my power back and forging a new path,

But I'll never forget you and the love we had.

For a time, it was us, it was beautiful and it was love.

That'll always be how I remember it.

Here's to new chapters and happy endings ...

Sometimes, you just have to know when to make new memories and let the old stuff go.

Maybe the next door that opens will be different ... that's all I can hope for.

That, and for you to be happy ...

Such is the way our stories go sometimes.

The Difference Between Having Love and Being Loved

She knew her worth and had promised herself long ago never to settle for anything less than what she deserved –
In her life, in her career, and most of all, in matters of the heart.
Sure, she'd made some bad choices and tried to mold the wrong guys into the right man, but she soon realized her mistakes.
You can't create a true love story if you're hoping he will change, so she stopped pressing and started to trust …
That meant to be will always find a way.
She didn't want just anyone or any kind of love, she wanted the one ...
The man who could see past her walls into her soul, the one who would engage her mind and enchant her heart.
No, just finding love would never satisfy her craving for the passionately deep love that would calm her yearning soul.
She needed more.
She deserved more.

She now understood why letting go of control was so much harder ...

She wanted to make it happen in love just as she had in the rest of her life ...

But she realized that true love was indeed magical, the stuff of fairy tales and dreams anon.

She couldn't manufacture love in any meaningful way, so she stopped trying and started focusing on what she could control: Herself.

She poured herself into becoming the best version of her that she could possibly be.

She stopped worrying about finding romantic love and started developing a love for herself that she had never truly known.

She began to find happiness in her own company and finally understood that being alone didn't mean she had to be lonely ...

Just the contrary.

It gave her the chance to evolve, improve and enjoy herself in a way that she had never grasped before.

Truthfully, she soon began to find peace in all the things that once scared her ...

She could dine alone, travel alone and anything else she chose … alone and perfectly content.

Her own company was the best companionship she'd ever had – and she no longer cared or worried if anyone else wondered why she was eating by herself.

What they thought didn't matter … how she felt was the most valuable truth that she'd ever uncovered.

Forget holding out for a hero, she became the heroine in her story.

Fairy tale ending or not, she was writing her chapters just the way she wanted …

On her terms, for her happiness.

Flying high and beautiful …

She was finally happy …

Love would show up when it was time, not a moment before … she finally understood the way it all worked.

Until then, she would chase her dreams and listen to her heart …

Always strong, wild and free.

May You Always Know the Beauty of Survival

My wish for you is that you never forget who you are and what amazing things you're capable of achieving.
May you always remember your inner fire and find your courage when you need it most.
I hope that you know that when the storms rage into your life you're never alone.
You're surrounded by love and the people who care about you, and there's never going to be a time that you'll have to stand alone.
My wish for you is that you always keep that gleam in your eye, fire in your heart and sparkle in your soul ...
For that is your wonderful magic that nothing and no one can ever take away from you.
Don't forget how strong your wings are, to carry you aloft to the places past the horizon, where the stars shine and your dreams will come true.
You were always made to soar, so never let anyone cage your spirit or dull your sparkle.

The world will try to dim your light, because most will never understand how beautiful your illuminating spirit is.

May you rekindle your passion often as you envision impossible dreams and seek the sunlight, because you were never meant to be ordinary.

I hope you find strength when life brings you to your knees, fighting back to reclaim your voice and take back your joy.

Your bravery will always lead you to those places where you will find purpose, passion and fulfillment.

Most of all, I want you to do more then to live or simply exist ...

I want you to thrive, to overcome your limits and redefine everything you thought you were ... Because you're capable of being so much more than you've ever realized.

You'll be beautiful when you survive the fire that threatens to tear you apart ...

Amazingly gorgeous when you rise again stronger, born anew from the ashes.

Sometimes you have to forget what you were to become what you're meant to be.

Today, as in all the other days to come,

you're beautiful, you're strong and you were
born to shine.

One Person Can Teach You That All People Are Not the Same

I realize that when I see the hurt behind your eyes, I'm only uncovering a very small part of your story.

Your gaze speaks volumes, and the whisper of your soul utters a thousand words I will never forget.

Yet, I know that I've only seen a glimpse of the person who lies hidden beneath the surface.

You've protected your heart because of all the ones in your past who tried to do more than hurt you, they wanted to control who you were.

The weak will always seek to reduce and diminish the strong, but you were better than that, smarter than them.

They never really got close enough to the soul behind the mask to take away your identity or break your spirit.

But it's made you so very cautious and hesitant to seek love again, and rightly so.

They hurt you because, deep down, you wanted to believe that they were different.

But until someone comes along who sees past the facade, behind your walls and through to

your soul, all the others will always be the same ...
Until me.
I know you don't need to be saved, completed or fulfilled.
You simply long to be loved, respected and appreciated for the person you are, the road you've traveled and the person you've worked hard to become.
But to truly comprehend the depths of you, it takes more than a day, week or a month:
It takes a lifetime ...
And I'm willing to dive deeply into your truths and unravel the secrets you've tucked away ...
However long it takes.
Each level of your hidden beauty unveiled only gives way to a deeper and more wondrous truth.
You've been waiting a long time to reveal who you really are to someone,
even longer to trust someone with every aspect of your heart.
I'm willing to be as patient as it takes, to slowly help you take down your walls to reveal the most precious parts of your heart ...

You're worth that and so very much more to me ...

Truth is, I've searched all my life for the person who my soul would recognize in the passing of a second.

You're my soul mate – my person, who I've known since before I knew of anything else –
I just hadn't found you yet in this lifetime.

I wish your broken road hadn't hurt you,
I wish that all the ones before weren't lessons, but as our paths were always meant to converge, I know now that this was always the road we were meant to travel.

It hasn't been easy, there will always be hard days, but it will all be worth it in the end.

After all, once in a lifetime is worth any road, no matter how long or broken.

One man, one woman, one love.

Your smile and embrace tell me that you finally feel the one thing the others never could make you feel:

Safe.

As I look in your eyes, I can feel my heart smile as the single thought comes to me.

I've finally found where I belong, in this life, with you.

Overthinking Will Not Just Kill Your Mind but Also Your Magic

There are so many times when I wish I could just shut my mind off.
The nights when I lay in bed, staring at the ceiling just … thinking.
I turn everything over and over in my mind, every possible reason, scenario, future and possibility.
I ask why and why not, even wonder what else could happen to change the things I'm thinking about.
Truth is,
I don't like being this way – overthinking is not a blessing and it never just goes away.
It's just how I'm wired and as have been for as long as I can remember.
Sometimes at night, they're demons that prey upon my worst fears.
Other times, they're angels that dance with me, celebrating the excitement of whatever I'm looking forward to.
One way or another, I'm never alone as I'm lost in thought … it never stops, and the silence can be deafening sometimes.

Often, I wish I could be like everyone else: just go to sleep and drift off peacefully into slumbering dreams.

That's when I stop and remind myself that I'm unique, and I smile feebly as I try to convince myself that there's a reason I'm this way.

The overthinking sometimes grows into insecurities that manifest in the worst possible ways –

Causing problems with others that never needed to happen.

My thoughts can create doubt in my head, tinge my magic and permeate the love in my heart if I don't stop them.

I wish I had a button that I could push whenever my mind overwhelms me, but unfortunately, it doesn't work that way.

I'm all those things that show how much I care about my people – I wouldn't change the size of my heart,

Because that's part of the magic that makes me wonderfully unique.

Yes, my mind can get the best of me sometimes, but I've learned to not let the overthinking control me anymore.

I know now that my power is my passionate love for the people in my life, and while I may worry about them a little too much, it's just who I am.

Maybe I overthink sometimes,

But I also over care, I overcome and, most of all, I over love.

I think the world needs more of that, so that's just what I'll do.

I just have to remind myself that everything else will work itself out the way it's supposed to.

And until then, I'll just keep loving hard when there's love to be had and make the best of all the rest.

What's meant to be will always find a way.

Silence Is a Woman's Loudest Cry

It's never her words that will tell you her story,
But her silence that speaks volumes.
Sometimes, rest cannot heal a weary heart,
though her mind is alive and spirited ...
Yet her depths are bone tired in a way that
sleep cannot remedy, nor could she explain if
she wanted.
Her eyes scream her truths where her words
sometimes do not, she hides all of her anguish
and love behind the walls she's built to protect
herself.
She's overcome heartache and struggle with a
soul forged of fire and a courage born of
necessity, so don't expect her to tear down her
walls easily.
She's fought for who and what she has, so
she'll break her ship upon the shore of solitude
before she ever allows someone close to her
heart who doesn't deserve her.
So, when you hear what she says and try to
understand her words, just know that her
unspoken truth is her greatest pride and most
fiercely prized part of herself.

She'll put on a brave smile and a gentle facade because that's how she survives some days – on pure bravery and strength of will.

She didn't choose to be the way she is, life pushed her across a broken road that she learned to survive and somehow, she found a way to thrive in the process.

Truth is, she doesn't want or need anyone to understand who she is behind closed doors … her heart is just too fragile to risk being broken again.

Deep down, she wants to love, but she's afraid the next person will be just like the last one who left her broken.

So, she's content to live her life and celebrate her small victories along the way.

She doesn't need fanfare or attention to be happy, she just needs contentment, peace and serenity.

So, before you knock on the door to her soul, know that she's a beautiful mess and a wonderful disaster, and she'll never be easy ... But one thing is for certain.

Her soulful depths and passionate love are unforgettable ... and no matter what,

She'll be worth any price you may have to pay
... To uncover the true beauty of a woman.

Your Laugh Reminds My Heart That We Have Already Fallen

Our meeting was never simply chance,
We were always meant to be.
The universe conspired to create our love,
A union since long forged in the stars above.
Across countless times and lifetimes past,
Our souls have always found each other,
Regardless of the distance or struggle.
We always have and will be together in love.
You became the dream that filled my nights,
The face without a name before ever meeting,
I knew of you intimately before our souls
collided … you were always meant to be my
true love.
As I lose myself in your eyes tonight,
A glimmer of love and lives past rekindles
And my heart stirs as I remember us from
before.
Soulmates, twin flames and true love.
In your smile, I see the warmth that I have
missed.
In your arms, the embrace that calls me home.
In your laugh, the sweet serenade of your love.

And in your kiss, the reminder of our never-ending love story,
Evermore.

Thank You for Loving Me When I Still Tasted of War

When you found me, I was an utter mess –
Completely broken and without joy.
I wasn't much fun to be around, and I couldn't see through my darkness.
I had lost the joy of living and couldn't dig my way out of the hole of loss and anguish I had buried myself in.
But you showed me that love isn't full of just heartache and pain … that there's a different side of love that I had never felt before.
I know you've been here through it all, and I just wanted to say thank you.
You've been patient with my fragile heart and held my hand through the hard days ...
Even wiped away my tears as I cried.
I thought heartache would destroy me, and it truly might have if you hadn't shown up when you did.
Your selfless love and undying devotion to my broken soul started to show me how to let the light in again.

You loved me when I didn't love myself and showed me kindness without expectation … something I had never known.

I'm sure I would have found my way eventually, but you led me from a place of love ...

And I don't think "thank you" will ever truly encompass how very deeply I care about you. It's been a long journey with a lot of down days, but you've never backed down or disappeared a single time, though I'm sure it wasn't always easy ...

I was a disaster for the longest time … and not the beautiful sort.

You didn't just help me put the pieces of my broken self back together, you held my hand as you patiently showed me the way back to myself.

You reminded me of my strength when I didn't have the courage to look for it myself.

I couldn't face the demons that haunted my thoughts at night, but you danced with them, distracting them in a way that somehow gave me peace … if only for a time.

So, as I look into the eyes of your beautiful soul, I'm overwhelmed with the blessing that I found in you.

You were everything I never knew I needed,
and you gave me a safe haven from my
storms.
You loved me when I didn't know how to love
myself, and for that and so much more,
I'm going to spend the rest of our lives showing
you just how very special you are to me.
Thank you for being here through it all, loving
me unconditionally,
And most of all, showing me how to love
myself when I had forgotten how.
You're my one true thing,
Now and for always.

I Hope You Find a Love That Inspires Dancing Instead of Walking on Eggshells … That You Are Able to Breathe Deeply Instead of Holding Your Breath

I hope you find the one-of-a-kind love
That fills your heart with joy and
Soothes your soul with absolute peace ...
The embrace that finally feels like home.
I hope you do all the things that make you feel alive:
Dancing in the kitchen making dinner,
Cuddling on the couch watching the rain,
Falling asleep together on lazy Sunday afternoons.
I hope you find the kind of amazing love
That leaves you breathless after kisses,
Making countless memories out of the moments
That will ever warm your heart across your lifetime.
I hope that together, you chase your dreams,
Face the storms side by side,
Take the trips to seek new adventures and

Create the life and love you've always
deserved.
Most of all, my wish for you is that you find the
person
Who makes you better than you ever thought
possible,
Who lifts you up and makes you stronger,
Able to walk hand in hand towards forever.
And most of all,
I hope you find the one ...
Who inspires you to fall in love with them
Each and every day for the rest of your lives.

I Am Brave and Untamed

I know that I'm not easy to love, sometimes
downright challenging at times.
My passionate disposition and my fierce heart
create a tangled web of love and strength that
can be hard to navigate.
I wear my emotions on my sleeve, and I always
speak what's on my mind.
Some people say I'm too proud or too full of
attitude for their taste, and I'm never going to
be everyone's favorite flavor.
It takes a connoisseur of strong women and
passionate hearts to appreciate all of me for
who and what I am.
Weaker men will scoff and say I'm too much,
too wild or too stubborn.
They just don't know how to be equal to a
brave woman ...
And I'm not wasting my time teaching a boy
how to be a man.
I've got a soul full of scars, and I've been
healing a broken heart for some time now, but
that's just part of my journey.

That doesn't define me nor does it weigh me down – I'll always be able to fly high with these wings forged in the fires of my struggles.

I'm not asking anyone to fix me, save me or heal my brokenness.

I just want real and lasting love.

Not the kind based on looks, make believe or a fairy tale.

There are no white picket fences in my story, I fell and broke those a long time ago.

No, I need the authentic, deep and passionate sort of love story between two equal parts of the same soul.

Someone to hold my hand through the storms, to dance with me in the rain and lose themselves by my side on adventures to nowhere.

It won't always be glamorous, nowhere close to perfect and it'll be full of mistakes, but it will be real.

I'm brave enough to lay it all on the line for fiery passion and strong enough to withstand the challenges that will come our way.

Most of all, I just want the love, respect and devotion of a partner who understands me in the ways that truly matter.

The person who can complete my thoughts and can decipher unspoken words with a single glimpse.

I crave a lover who won't try to tame me, but who will support me as I chase my dreams.

Real and lasting love is what I want and need, and I'm not settling or sacrificing for anything less than what I deserve ...

The one who will know from the very first moment we meet that I always meant to fly high ... and soars with me.

That's real, that's true and that's my plan for all my tomorrows.

A Big Part of Loving Yourself Is Knowing When to Let Go

Deep down, part of me knew that you really didn't ever love me the way I deserved.
I lied to myself for so long, trying to convince myself that this was it, that our love was the one I had always searched for.
I sacrificed so much of who I was as I tried to make our love into something that it was never meant to be.
I think you tried to love me in the best way you knew how, but I know now that was never going to be enough for me ...
Your love was never going to be enough.
I pretended that I was okay fighting for your attention, but the truth was, I could never accept being just an option for you.
So, I forgive you as I walk away, knowing that you never meant to hurt me.
It's my fault for not loving myself enough to stop settling and to start fighting for what I deserve ...
So that's what I'm doing now –
I'm standing up, I'm speaking up ... stating my mind and starting to reclaim my faded soul.

I realize that you're not part of my happily ever after, and that's okay.

You're the chapter that pushed me to remember who I am and what I want.

I had to be truly lost to know that I needed to start looking for myself again.

You taught me so much about myself that I couldn't have learned any other way.

You've helped me rediscover the parts of myself that I lost along the way.

I'm taking back my power and setting my heart on fire.

I know what I want and what I need, and I'm never again going to accept anything less.

I don't need to be perfect or for my life to be easy to find happiness,

But I do need to be loved for who I am the way I deserve ...

I will wait for the one who will see past my eyes into my soul and who knows my worth.

I'm not holding out for a hero; I'm saving myself the best way I know how.

By loving myself in the way I always should have ... And letting the rest take care of itself.

Some things are worth fighting for,

Most of all ... me.

I Would Use the Stars to Count the Ways I Love You, but Then, There's Not Enough Stars

I always longed to find the person who would fall in love with my smile,
the one would adore me even when I snorted and cackled when I laughed.
Many times, I thought I had found true love ... only to be left holding the pieces of my broken heart.
The fall from love was infinitely harder than falling into it.
And soon, you start to lose hope that you'll ever really find your person.
The "one" seemed impossible to find as my efforts to seek love always ended in failure.
I couldn't solve the riddle of the heart until,
In the blink of an eye, you changed everything for me.
All the others never really saw me for me until you glimpsed into my soul the very first time we met ...
The real, goofy and deep person I was didn't scare you like it did the ones before you.

In fact, it only drew you closer to me, and slowly, you started tearing down the walls around my heart.
I watched you smile and laugh with me every day,
and soon, it became very clear –
the epiphany of my love's journey was right in front of me.
You loved me for me – honest and real, without judgement or conditions.
Tears flooded my eyes as awe struck my heart.
How did you see what all the others had missed?
You engaged my mind, stoked my passions and whispered to my soul.
All along, it was always meant to be you ...
I knew you were the one from our very first smile,
I felt you were the one from our very first embrace.
You gave rhyme to my reason and hope to my tomorrows.
You were my one wish once made on a shooting star,

Dreaming that a love like yours could ever find me in a world full of broken roads and shattered hearts.

Truth be told, I'd say I could use the stars to count the ways that I love you,

But then, I'd run out of stars.

So, until they create a word that combines all the amazing and wondrous things that encompass my feelings for you,

I'll just stick with three.

I love you.

That's the best start to a life together and a better love story than I could have ever imagined.

Me and you, for always.

There's nowhere else I'd rather be

Than in your arms, for the rest of our days.

In a World Full of Dandelions, She Was and Always Would Be a Beautiful Rose

She was always the one that everyone called different.

They didn't understand her, and they didn't try to.

Her story was filled with quiet days and lonely nights, being cast aside by the people who just thought she was weird.

Sure, she'd always been quirky, unique and had her own style, but that's who she was.

She didn't ask anyone to like her, and she just walked away from the whispers about her "strangeness."

While the others spent their time fretting about how to best conform, she embraced her individuality and uniqueness.

It was hard, sometimes, being the one who everyone left out, but she learned long ago how to make peace with the struggles that accompanied being one of a kind.

She'd rather be marching to her own beat than following the crowd.

There was no joy for her in being the one who always did her own thing, but she was a woman of principle who would die an original than live as a copy.

She knew, as surely as the sun rose and set, that one day, the very same ones who mocked her quirky authenticity would celebrate those exact things about her ...

That was how she made it through the long nights and kept her resolve ...

And one day, when she opened her door to a sheepishly smiling young lady, her heart smiled ... People were finally wanting to be her friend – because some, perhaps only a few, appreciated her individuality and her strength to stand alone.

She wouldn't treat them as they did her – she was better than that.

She would embrace the ones who welcomed her friendship and loved her for who she was. Her kindness, loving heart and deep soul were the qualities that helped her rise above the feelings of never being accepted before.

They sought her out now for the very qualities they once scorned ...

And she showed them that only love can drive out hate ... In a world full of dandelions, she was and always would be a beautiful rose.

The Strength of My Soul Was Born on the Backs of Moments that Brought Me to My Knees

My journey has not been easy, but then, I own every experience along the way that has made me who I am.

The good, the bad and the ugly have built me up, broke me down and inflamed my heart like an ordinary path never could.

I've come to realize that I'm not defined by the moments that brought me to my knees, but rather how I rose again after falling.

I know now that I'm always going to make mistakes, have hard days and endure stormy times.

But I'll charge into those obstacles and turn them into opportunities.

My heart is alive with the fire that has forged my strength through the tough times, and my soul is full of my rising from the ashes.

I'd rather burn it all down than to fail … I'm not going out like that. I was meant for much more than to wallow in the dark and lament my struggles.

Give me the courage to always embrace the storms of today. Give me the passion to feel alive in all that I pursue. Give me the serenity to understand my journey and the truth of who I am.

I'll never be the baddest, the toughest or the fiercest, but I'll never quit, I'll always be real, and I'm going to embrace all my triumphs and tragedies.

This is my life and my story, and I'm choosing to live each and every day like the blessing that it is.

It takes sadness to understand happiness, failures to comprehend victory and chaos to know peace. Rain or shine, I'm doing it all by terms in my own way.

I'll never be perfect, and I'm good with that.

I know I'm amazing just the way that I am.

After all, the strength of my soul was born on the backs of the moments that brought me to my knees.

It was my spirit and soul that gave me the courage to rise again.

And now, it's my wings that will help me fly higher than ever before.

Strong, alive and free.

Finding the Small Miracles Among the Ordinary

I want to do all the things I've never done with you by my side.
I want to roll the windows down and let the wind blow through my hair.
I want to turn the music up and feel it permeate my soul as we chase adventure in obscure places and enjoy the beautiful serenity of peaceful retreats.
Let's soak in the wonder of those moments when we find the open road, a forest trail or hidden alcove where our dreams can come alive.
Let's hide away, if only for a bit, and escape the commotion of life.
I want to take in the history of places we've never been, enrich my mind in ways I've never done and always keep growing, learning and evolving.
I know there will days when I'll be a feisty handful and a complete mess, but that's just part of my unique charm ...
Or at least that's what I'm going with.

Those are the days I just need you to hold my hand and feed me chocolate.

It won't solve any problems, but it will make me feel better when I need it most.

You'll won't always know why I'm upset or even the reasons why I'm in a tizzy, but you don't have to.

I don't even understand myself sometimes – but those are the times I need you to love me hardest ... when I'm struggling.

Let's steal away moments at night when the world is slumbering to enjoy the quiet of our time together.

Relaxing in a tub while you read aloud our favorite love story will always be one of my most treasured memories,

The times where we leave the world behind and connect ... your soul and mine.

I want to live each day to its fullest, finding the small miracles among the ordinary that make our hearts smile.

Let's turn our faces to the sunlight and leave the wind at our backs, experiencing the joys that challenge our minds, fill our hearts and enrich our souls.

Forget the ordinary – I want out of the labels,
the boxes and expectations of who I should be
... Let's redefine ourselves and discover what
makes us feel extraordinary.

I want more than to just exist, let's fall in love
with being alive every day.

We will always have time to rest, spending
those days wrapped up in the cocoon of our
loving embrace ...

So, when life gives us the chance to chase our
dreams and live in the moment, let's seize
those opportunities with relentless optimism
and reckless abandon.

We never know what tomorrow will bring, so
let's enjoy today for the wonderful gift that it is
... Let's love with zealous passion, live with
fierce purpose and always follow our hearts.

You, me and forever ... we will always be truly
alive just past the horizon to our dreams.

My Greatest Regrets Have Come from Times When I Silenced My Heart and Let Fear Win

I know that I can never go back and change the past, so I've had to make peace with the regrets I have.
I wish I hadn't spent so much time trying to convince people that I was worthy.
Once, I was willing to settle for love on the terms of others who never really deserved me.
I should have never apologized for being myself, but a weaker and younger me wasn't strong enough yet to fight for her own voice, Unapologetically and courageously.
It always hurt when they broke my heart, and it made me think the problem was me.
I questioned what I did wrong, if I was pretty enough or why I always ended being the one picking up the pieces of a shattered heart.
I know now that I never should have sacrificed who I was to make someone else happy.
Fear of being judged, letting them down or not being enough suppressed my voice and quieted my heart.

I realize now that I tried to love people who never really saw me at all.

I wasn't important to them, and they never made me or my love a priority.

That made me feel small and stole away my courage in a way that took me so long to rediscover.

I look back with so many regrets about all the things I should have said and done along the way, but I know now that those are the struggles that helped me find my way home ... To myself, to my soul, to my identity that I had lost in my failed attempts to find love.

I tried to love all the wrong people in all the wrong ways, but that taught me exactly what I didn't want in my life, my heart and my future.

As painful as the past was, I know it led me down the road to where I was always meant to be.

I found a healthier love of myself, knowing what I wanted and what I deserved.

If someone couldn't give me their best, I could finally do what I never could before: let them go.

I stopped fighting all the wrong battles for all the wrong reasons chasing the love of all the wrong people ...
I realize that now, and I'm choosing a different path ...
Choosing to love myself, what I want and the people who really see and love me.
Heartache and loss almost broke me, but they created all the cracks I needed to let the light in, and I'm so very thankful.
Now I know what I never did before:
I'm beautifully broken, I'm wonderfully unique and most of all,
I'm perfectly imperfect,
Just the way I am.

You'll Always Be Too Much or Not Enough Until You Meet the One

She heard the same excuses from all the men who walked away ...

She was always "too much" or "not enough" to them – or at least, that was what they said as they broke her heart … one after another.

Loving halfway or small was never her thing – she poured all of herself into it every time ...

And she was left holding the pieces of her broken heart when they vanished, as they always seemed to do.

Her friends would try to comfort her by reminding her that those men weren't the ones for her, but it didn't make the heartache any easier.

She'd see the happy couples all around her and she'd lament that there must be something wrong with her since it never worked out for her the same way.

She started questioning what she could do differently or how she could change to make men stay in love with her.

It's easier to think that the problem is with you than to realize that the issue lies with trying to kiss all the wrong frogs and hoping they're really the right prince ...

Because no amount of hoping is ever going to make the wrong ones be the fairy tale.

She soon realized that she had to love herself most of all, regardless of what all the dead-end lovers thought.

She wouldn't and couldn't change to be someone she wasn't ...

And moreover, she didn't want to be anyone other than who she truly was.

She finally realized that being true to herself was the most important thing of all, and

Slowly, she began to own that truth ...

No matter the opinion of those who didn't matter.

But, until destiny came calling, she didn't really know what she wanted or where to go next ...

Only that she wanted to be happy.

If that included love, so be it, but that wouldn't alter her life choices anymore.

That's the thing about love – it chooses all the details we wish we could control:

Who, when and how.

So, when he showed up unexpectedly in the most improbable way, all she could do was smile and shake her head.

He wasn't what she expected, nor could she have ever seen him coming, but that's the beauty of writing your own love story:

Each one is unique and wonderful in different ways – no two are ever the same.

So, as her eyes met his in a loving gaze, she realized why she was always too much or never enough for all the others before.

Meant to be has a way of making you forget all the mistakes and disappointments of loves past.

Her heart was full and her soul sighed as she finally knew ...

She had found her forever love ...

All of her broken roads had led her where she was meant to be – to him – and she wouldn't change a thing …

Other than she would have found him sooner so that she could have loved him longer ...

In a love story unique and wonderful in all the ways she would always cherish.

Her love, her way, her forever.

The Enchanting Cocoon of Your Loving Embrace

There's just something beautiful about the moment when I first reach your arms.

As your arms wrap around me for a warm embrace, time slows and the world melts away. No matter the day I've had nor the struggles I've endured, everything just seems right in those moments.

Honestly, if I could stay forever in your arms, I'd probably never leave the enchanting cocoon of your loving embrace.

The feelings that we exchange through those simple but powerful moments almost escape words, because it feels so amazing as I soak in your touch … your love … your soul.

They say it's the big moments that define our lives, but it's the little memories of being in your arms that will always linger in my mind and heart.

There's nothing I would ever change about us, except maybe that we could stay in each other's arms, forever.

There's no place I'd rather be than in your heart and arms, for always.

Brave Enough

For so long, I played it safe and hid my truth
behind a warm smile, a gentle laugh and a
quick wit.
I didn't want to risk the world invading my heart
and judging me for who I truly was.
Truthfully, that's what I thought everyone did –
that pretending was the easier path.
But after a time of stifling my authenticity,
hiding my soul behind placid eyes and
guarding my heart with ferocity, I just got tired.
Tired of living a life that wasn't me and never
would be.
Fear is a hard master – one not easy to break
free from.
I was absolutely afraid of what the world would
say about who I really was ...
Until one day, I realized it didn't matter what
anyone else said about me or my life.
My happiness was so much more important
than their opinion of me.
I was done living a lie,
It was time to embrace who I am and who I
was always meant to be.
I don't care what anyone says about how I

look, what I say or how I think.

It's my life and I don't need anyone's approval or acceptance to take control.

My happiness isn't dependent on anyone else – I forge my own path through the fires of life and how I swim in the depths of challenge.

There's always going to be days where my hair is a mess, my outfit isn't my favorite and I'm grumpy ...

But therein lies the beauty of taking back your power.

I own it all – the good, the bad and the ugly.

So, the bravery I found wasn't the kind that will win medals or change the world,

But it has changed my world, and that's what matters most.

Standing strong in my own light, turning my face to the sunlight and charging forth is who I am now, every day.

I know it won't always be easy, it won't ever be painless, but

I'm worth it, and I deserve to find my own happiness,

Just the way I want.

Regret

I know that I can never go back and change the past, so I've had to make peace with the regrets I have.

I wish I hadn't spent so much time trying to convince the people that I wanted to love me that I was worthy.

Once, I was willing to settle for love on the terms of others that never really deserved me.

I should have never apologized for being myself, but a weaker and younger me wasn't strong enough yet to fight for her own voice, Unapologetically and courageously.

It always hurt when they broke my heart, and it made me think the problem was me.

I questioned what I did wrong, if I was pretty enough or why I always ended being the one picking up the pieces of a shattered heart.

I know now that I never should have sacrificed who I was to make someone else happy.

Fear of being judged, letting them down or not being enough suppressed my voice and quieted my heart.

I realize now that I tried to love people that never really saw me at all.

I wasn't important to them and they never made me or my love a priority.
That made me feel small and stole away my courage in a way that took me so long to rediscover.
I look back with so many regrets about all the things I should said and done along the way, but I know now that those are the struggles that helped me find my way home ...
To myself, to my soul, to my identity that I had lost in my failed attempts to find love.
I tried to love all the wrong people in all the wrong ways, but that taught me exactly what I didn't want in my life, my heart and my future.
As painful as the past was, I know it led me down the road to where I was always meant to be.
I found a healthier love of myself, knowing what I wanted and what I deserved.
If someone couldn't give me their best, I could finally do what I never could before: let them go.
I stopped fighting all the wrong battles for all the wrong reasons chasing the love of all the wrong people ...
I realize that now, and I'm choosing a different

path ...

Choosing to love myself, what I want and the people who really see and love me.

Heartache and loss almost broke me, but they created all the cracks I needed to let the light in.

And I'm so very thankful.

Now I know what I never did before:

I'm beautifully broken, I'm wonderfully unique and most of all,

I'm perfectly imperfect,

Just the way I am.

Reclaiming My Voice

All the ones that left thought they knew what was best for me when they didn't know me at all.
They thought they could change who I was by sabotaging my courage, suppressing my voice and take away my identity.
I made the mistake of defining myself by us, not me.
I lost myself in the people I loved and forgot my truth by listening to their lies.
They tried to change me to what they wanted me to be in order to make themselves happy.
They never really loved me for who I was and somewhere along the way, I woke up and realized I wasn't okay with being devalued and dismissed.
My voice, my soul and my happiness matters … and it always will.
Sure, I was unsure what to do or where to go next, but I knew that something had to give.
I could no longer live by the approval and permission of another person,
Especially one who never really had my best interests at heart.

So, now, I'm reclaiming all the things that I let be stolen from me by people who were always going to walk away.

I'm finding more strength every day, and I'm digging myself out of the darkness just a little more, one small step at a time.

I'm tired of being a small candle … I'm going to find my flames again.

I'm coming back to who I was always meant to be … a roaring wildfire that cannot be extinguished.

My voice will be heard and I will own my happiness.

I will rise and I will fall, but I'll always do it on my terms, in a manner of my choosing.

No longer will I accept someone else's definition of who I am and what I should do.

I'm taking back all the things I lost along the way with a voice that does not shake.

I'm reclaiming my magic, rediscovering my strength and forging my path from the fires I've survived.

It won't always be easy, and I'll fail more than I'll succeed, but at least I'll own my fate in the end.

My soul will shine and my heart will be alive for

my life once again like it was before … them.
I've been lost for so long, finding my way back
won't be an easy journey.
But I'll never forget the fuel for my light that will
carry me higher than I've even been before.
I'm beautiful, I'm strong and most of all, I
deserve to be happy in the ways I choose.
I finally remembered my most important truth of
all …
Forget being "enough."
I'm worth it all, and I won't stop until I get it.
My way, on my terms.
This time, though, I'll be better, wiser and
stronger.
And I'll never look back.

A little girl once made a promise to herself that
she vowed to never forget:
To chase her dreams and stay beautiful inside
and out, no matter what challenges she faced.
She'd never lose the memory of who she was
and the vow she made ...
Regardless of success, failure or fame.
That same little girl became a striking woman,
successful and independent.
The difference between her and all the rest?
She didn't sell her soul to make it to the top.
She fought, clawed and sacrificed every step of
the way.
The most amazing part of this fierce woman?
She kept that little girl's promise to always
remain true to who she was.
She helped the others that the crowd shunned.
She picked up the fallen and carried them until
they could carry themselves.
Never forgotten were her beginnings,
Never lost was her vow made so long ago.
Those who crossed her path could only wonder
what it was that made this woman so deeply
beautiful.

The fact was, she had realized a long time ago that beauty – true beauty – wasn't something that depended on makeup, clothes or looks.
It would always be so much deeper than that ... deep and lasting beauty was the soulful kind ... and that's the most lasting and impactful beauty of all ...
The others may have mastered makeup, hair and clothes, but her inward beauty far outshined the rest.
She would always be beautiful in her heart and soul in the ways the others couldn't – and didn't understand.
She had that special something that defied description – the depth of her that many could never see.
The passion of her heart,
The radiance of her soul,
The courage of her spirit ...
You'd never mistake the fierce beauty that she was in all the ways that mattered most.
She didn't need fancy clothes or makeup to leave her mark on the people she touched ...
She was unforgettable to both men and women, the ones who glimpsed the sparkle in her eyes and brilliance of her soul.

If you ever met her,
And truly saw her for the person she was,
That's when you realized what most missed:
She didn't need a spotlight,
She shined from within.

Before You, I Never Knew What to Wish For

There was a time that seems so long ago,
That I didn't think love would ever find me.
Wishing on shooting stars, always hoping,
That someday, destiny would come calling.

I really didn't know what I wanted,
Other than the cliches that I had heard,
Because until real and lasting love finds you,
You don't know how powerful it truly is.

All the dreams and hopes I once had,
The ideals and desires melted away
Once your smile brightened my life,
And I realized that all I knew was wrong.

You showed me the true meaning of love,
How amazing life could be when you find
The one meant to be yours,
And forever takes on a completely new
meaning.

I never could have imagined the love I found in
you,

Nor the way you leave me breathless,
As you embrace me with a powerful love
That engulfs me and never lets me go.

And while I didn't know your name or face,
I now realize what I had known all along ...
It was always you that was meant for me,
As it will always be us, two that became one –

For my love story has finally smiled at me,
Bringing us to a place we shall never leave.
Until time is no more and forever ceases to be,
I'll always be loving you, endlessly.

I Am Worth More Than Your Second Thoughts and Maybes

I know what you thought about me, but you got
it all wrong.
I realize you thought I was like all the rest and
would be okay being just an option for you.
Not even close.
I know my worth and I'll never settle for
anything less than what I want.
I deserve the best from anyone in my life,
because that's what I give – my all ...
And that's exactly what I deserve …
everything.
I don't love small and I don't believe in halfway
anything –
Passion, love or happiness.
Life's too short for me to accept less what I'm
worth.
So, please save the maybes, possiblies and
second thoughts for someone else,
I'm not okay with playing games.
I may be too intense and strong willed for
some, but those aren't my people.
Give me the dreamers, the lovers and the
strong-willed warriors – they're the ones I'll go

through the fire for.

So, if you don't know what you want or have to think about my importance,

Then let's part ways as friends.

It's not fair to either of us to try to make something work that was never meant to be.

I learned a long time ago to accept that things have a way of working out if you respect yourself, others and destiny.

So, if you want to hold my hand through the storms, dance in the rain and chase your dreams with me by your side,

Then let's go find some adventures.

Rise or fall, rain or shine,

Let's love hard when there's love to be had.

The choice is up to us if we are meant to be just a chapter or perhaps, a happily ever after.

Forever doesn't accept maybes,

And neither will I.

Behind Every Strong Woman Is a Story That Gave Her No Other Choice

I never really had a choice on the person I became.

I went down all the broken roads and fell down so many times, I didn't know if I would ever get back up sometimes.

When you find all the doors closing and feel disappointment around every corner, you almost stop seeing the good things in your life.

It's easy to get stuck in all the bad stuff and even easier to wallow in it.

But I had a choice ...

Either stay in the darkness and accept being miserable, or rise above the struggle and forge an iron will that can't be broken.

Yes, my wings got clipped for a time.

Yes, I stumbled and fell to my knees.

Yes, I stopped being happy for a while..

But that's when I remembered who I was and that I was so much more than I had let myself become.

I'm not a failure even though I've failed.

I've made mistakes but that will never define me.

I'll stumble and fall, but I won't stay down –
ever.

I found myself in a black abyss that threatened
to overwhelm me.

However, that's how my story ends.

Yes, my tale has heartbreak and struggle,
failure and setbacks, but it is so much more
than that.

It's also full of chapters of fighting back, finding
my strength and rising from the ashes.

And while I can't go and change the mistakes
of the beginning, I hold the power to rewrite the
next chapters and create a happy future.

It may not be the prettiest tale of adventure,
love and dreams, but it will always be genuine,
authentic and real ...

Just like me.

Forget all the negativity that once dragged me
down, I'm forging a different direction.

One full of hope, love and dreams that will
resurrect my spirit in ways that, once, I didn't
think possible.

I know now what I never realized before:

I control my own destiny and it's up to me
where I end up and how.

I'm raising my voice, stoking my passion and

spreading my wings like I never have before.
This time, I'm reaching for the stars and never
looking back.
My life, my dreams.
Just like me, they're absolutely strong
and immeasurably beautiful.

I Want to Make Every Day a Wild Adventure

I woke up today and realized I needed more ...
More of all the things that matter most to me.
I want to be able to close my eyes, open my
heart and feel the magic in the moments that
I've been overlooking.
To see and hear the little things that have been
escaping me and to fall in love with being alive,
every day.
I know that there are still going to be rainy days
and painful times, but I control how I let those
things affect me.
I'm taking my spirit, my life and my power back.
I'll probably still think about things too much
and worry at night when I'm lying in bed, but
I'm done letting it control me.
I'm stepping back from the hustle of life and
everything I've let have too much importance.
It's not enough anymore to just take life day by
day.
I want to truly feel alive – heart, mind and soul.
I want to experience my soul brimming with
contentment while I enjoy life again.
I want to electrify my heart as I chase my

dreams and let passion permeate my spirit.
Every day may not be exciting, but I choose to find the joy in the ordinary moments and the love in the wonderful people that I surround myself with.

I'm changing my life, my world and most of all, my mindset.

I realize now that anything is possible if I believe.

I know that I can change everything if I stop living in the future and I start living in the moment.

Every day may not be great, but there's something great in every day.

It's up to me to find it.

With the wind at my back and sunlight in my soul, there's nothing I can't do ...

Starting with today, I'm going to shine brighter than ever before ...

My way.

Bestie, Soul Sister, Friend

As my phone lights up with your name, my heart smiles.
You've been there through it all, holding my hand through the storms and dancing with me through the victories.
We've always been close and our bond is so much than "friends."
In fact, I don't know of a word that begins to describe what you mean to me.
Bestie, soul sister, friend … our love for each other runs so much deeper than that.
No matter how long it's been, we always pick up like we've never missed a beat.
You're the first one I call when I'm falling apart and the person I want to celebrate with the most.
From the very first time we met, we just got each other.
A single look between us would speak volumes and there's nothing we won't talk about …
good, bad and ugly.
Friends are the family we choose, and since the very first day, we've been inseparable in spirit.

So, as I pick up your call and say hello,
happiness floods my spirit, because all is right
with the world in that moment.
Come what may, no matter the storms life
brings,
We will always have each other, through thick
and thin … and we always will.
That's just what we do, you and me ...
Laugh through the tears, cry though the
hilarious and protect each other in every way.
There's no other person that I'd rather share
my joy with than you ...
You make this thing called life a marvelous
journey ...
Hand in hand, there's nothing we can't do ...
And probably will, laughing hysterically along
the way.

Hiding and Calling It Lost

I tried for so long to hide from all the things I
didn't want to face.
I'd smile through the heartache and tears,
saying that I was just lost.
Truthfully, I'd make any excuse to bury the pain
and try to forget the past.
I thought it was easier to ignore what I was
feeling so I could attempt to create a safe
haven from my thoughts – though they never
seemed to stop running through my mind.
I hid from the truth with the hopes that I could
find a way through the memories ...
that I could avoid the reality of things I never
made peace with.
Nothing I tried ever worked out the way I had
hoped.
All I could do was buy myself moments of
respite from the buried pain and hidden
memories.
That's when I realized I couldn't run from the
past anymore if I wanted to ever truly build a
happy future.
I had to face my truths and confront my fears if
I hoped to find real and lasting peace.

All the excuses and claims of being lost never did anything but make me more anxious.

I realized that I had to stop hiding and start living my life if I wanted to be happy.

I still have days when I can't stop thinking about where I've been and there are many nights when the worries keep me awake.

Thankfully, each step along the way gets a little easier, and my heart finds a little more happiness as I edge a little further away from the pain.

There are still storms in my soul, but as long as I keep moving forward, they're not as often nor as intense.

There are more and more moments of hope and light the harder I push myself free of the chaos I once dwelled in.

I may never be able to completely put the past away, but then, I don't want to ...

those are the lessons I was always meant to learn along the way.

The good and the bad – the pain and the joy – each makes up a little piece of who I am.

I'm taking back my power and owning my magic.

I'm done hiding.

Now, I'm going to do what I should have all along:
Love and live on my terms ...
Finding myself has never been so beautiful ...
Each and every day,
the person that I'm seeing in the mirror now is
exactly who I was always meant to be:
Happy, free and truly alive.

Warrior Eyes and an Iron Will

You think you know who I am, but here's some truth for you.
You've never met a person like me and you never will again.
I don't talk, walk or act like the others, and I don't want to.
The world has plenty of copies and fakes, I choose to be different ...
Because I will always listen to my heart and march to my own beat.
I'm proudly original, and I tackle life with a style and ferocity all my own.
People who don't understand me will say I'm weird or have an attitude,
And that's what weaker people will think about the brave souls that shine brighter than the rest.
You knew from the moment our eyes met that I had the spirit of a warrior, heart of a lover and soul of a dreamer.
I won't be denied what I pursue, and I don't know how to quit.
It's not enough for me to just survive.
I overcome and thrive.

"Good enough" is something for everyone else. That doesn't mean I don't have hard days or an easy life, I just forged my will out of a courage born of fire, and I learned to overcome.

I rise when others fall and I smile through the tears, dance through the rain and keep moving forward.

I don't accept less than the best, and I'll never be okay with making do.

My heart is restless and my soul is deep.

Loving me isn't easy, but it's a glorious adventure and well worth the challenge.

You'll always know where you stand with me because my voice will always be heard.

Don't treat me like an option if you want to be a priority – I'm too strong, free and beautiful to chase anyone to be part of my life.

If you can't love me as an equal and treat me with respect, then you need to look elsewhere.

My passion is fiery and my devotion is fierce – I'll love you like a firestorm and kiss you like a hurricane.

There's no such thing as halfway in my world, so if you're unsure of what you want, then I'm not the one for you.

Sunlight or storm, you can always count on me

to stand strong by your side, holding your hand
while we embrace the day.
So, if you have stars in your eyes and
adventure in your soul, keep up – let's go
chase some forever.
Me, you and our dreams,
Just the way it was meant to be.
Dreams don't have deadlines and my love
doesn't come easy.
I'm strong, I'm beautiful and I'll always be
holding your hand …
Let's go find something wonderful together ...

There Are No Accidental Meetings
Between Souls

I've long since stopped trying to understand
How the universe brought us together.
There are larger forces at work in love
Than we can ever truly grasp.

Because when I see your beautiful smile,
I can't help but melt with adoration …
With the love that I found so beautifully
In you, for now and always.

I dreamed of you before ever we met.
I knew your face before I ever found you,
We were always meant to be,
In this life, we were the love story unending.

All my broken roads and lost loves
Shattered my heart in countless ways,
But as I take your face in my hands,
It all melts away before the splendor of our
love.

I know now that accidental meetings
Are not the way of love's story,

As our paths were always to have crossed,
One heartbeat and two souls, complete,
evermore.

I read all the love stories and thought I knew
What real and lasting love truly felt like,
But as our lips meet and our souls embrace,
I know now that nothing could ever compare
To the beautiful love that I found in you.

She Had a Very Inconvenient Heart … It Insisted on Feeling Things So Deeply

Everyone knew her, but no one really did.
She was much like the others, except that she felt everything so much deeper than anyone else.
She wasn't capable of shallow emotions or superficial feelings, something inside her just didn't work that way.
Her heart had the most unusual way of soaking in the feelings of those around her – she couldn't escape how deeply the emotions of others would resonate with her heart and soul. Most of her life, she thought everyone was just like her, until one day, she came across the word empath.
It explained so much about who she was and how she felt everything so deeply to her core. It even helped her understand the sensory overload that she would often experience around others …
Overwhelmed by their thoughts, feelings and words … she was often left drained in a manner well beyond physical.
Sometimes, you can't rest a tired soul through

sleep … it needs so much more than that.
Truth is, she didn't want to be that person who felt everything so deeply, she wished most days she could just wall off her heart to save herself from the draining emotions of others. She couldn't understand the purpose of such powerful depth until she began to try to understand herself better.

It was a lengthy journey of introspection that wasn't easy and was often painful … but what she knew she needed to find her peace.

What she needed most of all was balance – in how she felt, how she hurt and how she could stave off the unwanted emotions of others.

It didn't always work, but the more she tried, the stronger she became.

Suitors would come calling, thinking she was just another woman.

They never could grasp the depth that lie guarded behind her eyes.

She would never be the one comfortable with ordinary conversations about normal topics ... She needed much more than that.

She wanted the midnight talks that lasted for hours about soulful purpose and radiant love that most men weren't comfortable having ...

And she was more than okay with that: she didn't want most men.

She accepted and loved who she was and made her heart and needs very clear – she'd rather be alone than to be unfulfilled by another.

She didn't need anyone to make her happy, for she saw the world in a much different light than most ever would ...

In shades of vibrant hues and colorful passion that escaped most people.

She was content to escape into those beautiful moments, living fully and enjoying the surreal wonder of her existence.

She didn't just think, feel or love with an ordinary depth.

She was always meant for more, and she took solace in that during the harder times.

Some people were meant to believe, others designed to succeed ... she was going to shine differently than the rest.

She was one of the special few that felt the universe just the way it was intended.

She only knew how to live, love and dream in all the colors of the heart.

She was at peace, she was alive ...

And wherever she was, no matter how hard,
She always found a way to be happy.

Sometimes Brave Women Fall in Love with Weak Men

When I saw you across the street,
I found myself smiling –
The kind of grin that is thoughtful and wistful.
Not because I miss you or I'd change anything
about the life we once shared,
But because we will always have those
wonderful memories of a love that was never
meant to be.
We don't always choose who we fall in love
with, but the chapters we write are up to us …
mostly.
No matter how deeply we loved or the
promises we made, I learned it takes much
more than love to last forever.
Maybe it's written in the stars, maybe our
hearts know the truth all along, or maybe
destiny holds the cards of who makes it and
who doesn't.
I don't blame you for what happened, really,
because you loved me the best way you knew
how ...
But my spirit was too fierce and my passion too
intense for us to ever really have had a

chance.

You gave our love everything you had, but deep down, we both know you didn't truly understand my soul the way I needed.

You said you wanted a brave and strong woman, that you needed passion in your life, but along the way, the very things that drew you to me just pushed you away.

I wasn't ever meant to be tamed, controlled or watered down ...

You finally realized that I wouldn't ever be the woman you thought you needed all along.

In letting me go, though, you thought you broke my heart ...

But really you set me free.

To find who I really was and have the chance to meet someone else that loved and appreciated me just the way I am ...

Unconditionally.

So, as I see you across the way, my smile brightens as I think back to the times we had. You helped me become the person that I was meant to be, all along.

Thank you for loving and caring about me – you'll always have a place in my heart.

Most of all, you showed me that some people

were meant to be in your heart,
Not in your life.
Thank you for setting me free … to fly high like
I was always meant to,
Happy, strong and free.

Strong Women are Warriors with Hearts of Gold

I didn't choose the path I've had to walk,
It chose me.
Sometimes, you don't get a choice – you do
what you have to do to keep going.
You fight and struggle for so long, you stop
remembering that life can be any other way.
I stopped seeing the beauty of life all around
me because I had lost myself in the fight for my
survival.
I was no longer living, I was simply existing.
There comes a time when you have to step
back and remember who you are.
Fight for your purpose and stop going through
the motions.
I was done living day to day and holding my
breath waiting for the next disaster.
I'm meant for more than that.
I've not only survived the flames, I've become
the fire.
No more holding on by a thread; instead, I'm
attacking my days with intense passion and a
fully awakened soul.
Somewhere along the way, I chose to stop

being miserable, and I decided to choose happiness.

I'm not saying I don't have hard days and don't cry in the shower sometimes, but I learned to elevate what I would accept from of my life.

Forget trying to dance in the rain and celebrating the storm, give me the sunlight and show me the way to beautiful moments.

I'm still going to worry about all the things I can't control, and I'll probably still lay awake in bed thinking about everything and everyone.

Being strong doesn't mean I am carefree and easy going ...

It means I can handle anything my life throws at me.

I'm not a survivor, I'm a warrior.

I forged my mettle in the fires of struggle and rose stronger out of the ashes of my failures.

I love hard and live passionately, and I won't ever settle or be demeaned.

My life, my terms, my joy.

I'm letting the rest go while I chase my dreams.

I'm not easy to love, but I'm worth it.

I give everything my all, and I don't accept anything less than the best ...

From my people, from myself and from love.

I'm not playing the game, I'm rewriting the rules
on who I am and what I want.
But, through it all,
at the end of the day,
What I want is very simple.
I just want to be happy,
strong and soulfully alive ...
The way I choose, on my terms.
Rain or shine, I'm going to be at the top,
Shining bright and smiling.

How Do You Go Back to Being Strangers with Someone Who Has Seen Your Soul?

I thought I could just forget you ...
That the pain of losing you wouldn't hurt so badly ...
But I was wrong.
I wanted to bury the feelings we once shared in a place where they wouldn't cut me anymore ...
But that's impossible.
I knew I'd never truly heal if I didn't face my pain.
Of all the things you told me, I just can't forget how you said you would always be there.
Promises of loyalty have now faded away to forgotten words.
You made it seem easy when you walked away, like what we had just didn't matter ...
But it does.
It always will.
I can't just forget someone who meant so very much to me like they didn't even exist,
Even if you can, I can't and won't.
I'll always cherish what we had, because it beautiful in its time, in its way.

I learned so much from you and because of you, I'd never change anything.

I forgive you for the anguish you caused, because I'm better than holding onto the past, No matter how painful.

Dwelling on what happened between us and over-analyzing what went wrong didn't do anything for me but cause me sleepless nights and countless tears.

Truth is, I'll never really know why you quit on us or how you could turn your back on me seemingly so easily.

I've had to make peace with the fact that you were never meant to be my person, and though it hurt so badly, it's gotten better as the days have passed.

There were so many days when I didn't want to get out of bed and I ignored everyone's calls.

I couldn't see the light for the darkness I tried to blame on you ...

That's when I woke up and realized you couldn't help the way you were, and we can't change what's meant to be.

People come into your life for a season, a reason or a lesson ... and you were all three for me.

You made me remember how strong I was before you, no matter how hard the challenges life threw at me.

As I look at your picture on my phone, a sad wistful smile creeps into the corners of my mouth … because I know I should thank you … For setting me free, for reminding me of who I am,

And most of all, forcing me to find a way through the pain of heartbreak.

I'm stronger now than I've ever been.

It may be some time before it gets easier, but every day that passes, I get a little stronger … A little wiser.

A little happier.

It's strange thinking that later in my life, I'll look back and you'll be just another person that passed through, a chapter that closed ever so painfully …

But that's the thing about my story.

It's just getting started, and I've got sparkle in my eyes again.

My soul is remembering how to be alive once more.

This time, I'm taking the pen and writing my story just how I should have all along.

With passionate love, soulful life and
unbreakable purpose.
I'm doing it all my way ...
Because now,
More than ever ...
I'm beautiful, I'm strong and I'll always be
unbreakable.

Vulnerability

He took a deep breath and closed his eyes,
embracing his chance – and his choice –
to finally be himself.
All his life, he'd been told how he should act
and what he should do.
Whether it was older men, friends or even
strangers, everyone always seemed to have an
opinion on what constituted a "real man."
Men weren't supposed to cry – that was a sign
of weakness. Men weren't supposed to be
vulnerable, that wasn't how tough men acted.
Men weren't supposed to show the world who
they were truly were, lest they be judged.
After a great deal of soul searching, he knew
the only way to be truly happy was to embrace
his fully aware and alive self.
He was miserable trying to fit into the boxes of
what the world said he should be.
No more, he could no longer be what others
thought he should be.
He was through living to please everyone else
… he was finally discovering the path to his
own happiness in the ways that mattered to
him.

He had finally come to that place where he could no longer pretend to be something he wasn't.

A solitary tear trailed down his cheek as he felt his heart begin to beat fervently.

He was taking control of his life, owning who he was, and he didn't care what anyone else thought.

They didn't feel his pain, know his struggles or walk in his shoes.

He didn't live by their leave, and he didn't need anyone's approval of the way he pursued happiness.

Yes, he knew he did all the things that tough guys weren't supposed to do:

He cried at the sappy movies, he expressed his emotions and he wasn't afraid to acknowledge his weaknesses.

The way he saw it, the very thing that the others would say made him weak would make him strongest of all.

He took back his power and, with it, control of his destiny and happiness.

It was then that he knew he could finally become the man he was meant to be all along – Emotionally aware, strong and free ...

Maybe not in the ways that everyone always thought a man should be, but in all the truest sense of the word.
Never again would he let others control how he thought or change how he acted.
Most of all, he could finally love with all his heart in the way he had always wanted to ...
Himself, his friends and most of all, whomever his heart chose.
He smiled at the thought.
This time, it was only up to him,
His choices, his heart, his way ...
And he never looked back.

This is for the many men who have expressed that men fight the same emotional battles that woman do – And they do, but so many have a different battlefield of struggle, as the world has tried to dictate what is "acceptable."
This goes out to the amazing men out there who embrace their feelings, express their vulnerability and know they're stronger for it ...
No matter what anyone says.
The world needs more men like that –
Alive, aware and strong in the ways that matter.

Believe in Magic

When he told me the story, I couldn't believe
magic was real.
I wouldn't believe that anything – or anyone –
held such power.
That was the stuff of old wives' tales and
children's stories, and reflecting back to the
wise old man who spun a yarn of a woman
who had once stolen his heart,
I still found myself shaking my head.
I thought to myself very assuredly,
"People like that don't exist."
It was cute to hear his words of her magical
ability to change his world and his heart for the
remainder of his days, but I scoffed at the
veracity of such a tale.
You know, we always doubt anything that
sounds too good to be true … until it happens
to us.
The old man never would have been able to
make me understand how love was magic …
he always just told me "you'll know when you
find it."
I had long since written off his fairy tale as
foolishness.

That is, until the magic came calling my name one day.

I didn't have to ask who you were, hear you speak a word, or even know your name.

From that split second you turned to face me, eyes locked for the first time in our lives,

I knew exactly what the old storyteller had been talking about.

As your deep hazel eyes drew me in with alluring captivation,

all thoughts fled my mind, and I could only exist in that moment, with you.

I can't describe it even to this day when your arms are around my neck, when our lips meet in a soft kiss,

only that you are that magic that I had never believed in.

The very first time I saw you smile, nothing else was ever the same, and I wouldn't have it any other way.

How can one person come into your life and change it forever?

Well, the way I see it, there's only one explanation that fits.

Magic ... in every way possible ...

How they moved, the look in their eye, every

little thing they said or did.
More than simple magic … it was love –
And just like the magic I had once doubted,
it was real, it was beautiful and it was forever.

Tilting Your Face to the Sun

Today, I made a promise to myself.

Instead of focusing on what I'm doing tomorrow or worrying about what the future may hold, I'm going to start living fully in the moment.

I always thought I was living that way until I noticed all the little things I had missed along the way.

Sure, I caught all the important stuff, but I realized I was totally overlooking all the intangible magic that was hidden in the moments.

The kind smile of a stranger, the way the sunlight warms my face, the smell of rain after a midday storm … the things I wouldn't notice before because I wasn't really paying attention. I thought I was until one day, a picture captured a beautiful memory that I was present for … but not really there.

That was my awakening, and the day my decision was made to begin being present, living every moment to its fullest and letting the magic of the world around me permeate my soul. To truly be in love with being alive, I soon understood, that's what it would take to enjoy

the beauty that unfolded each and every day.
At first, I thought it would be easy to always be present until the draw of life tried to pull me away. The allure of all those things that I used to lose myself in for hours was the reason I hadn't been experiencing life the way I truly wanted to.

The less I zoned in on the screens, the distractions and the mind-numbing media, the more I noticed life's beauty in moments both big and small.

Learning to balance the need for life's essentials and the desire to live in the moments allowed me to soak in the things that electrified my passions and filled my soul.

In the end, I learned that I didn't need grand adventures to faraway lands to be happy and enrich myself.

I just needed to unlearn all the behaviors that took me away from living in the now.

I'll always have worries about tomorrow and there will always be distractions, but with love in my heart and passion in my soul,

I'll do what I had so often missed out on before ... I'll fall in love with being alive in all the moments, every day.

If You Were Lying Next to Me

There are those times at night when I look over at the empty place in the bed beside me and try not to cry.
I fight back the tears because I can't let the dam break … or I'll be crying for hours.
Maybe it's loneliness, maybe I miss you,
Or maybe it's a little bit of both.
Truthfully, I don't really know.
All I do know is that my thoughts run wild with the flashes of the memories we made together and the love we shared.
I always knew that nothing is forever, but I wish so very much you were lying beside me ...
Breathing as you slept, peacefully quiet as the serenity of night enveloped us in a protective cocoon.
I'd snuggle up to you and smile as your eyes would open –
The corners of your mouth would curl into that smirking smile I so adored, and I'd lean in and kiss you.
You'd ask me wistfully why I was awake, and I would try not to blurt out every random thought had crossed my mind for the last few hours ...

I'd smile warmly and just say, "you know, stuff on my mind."

Those are the memories that come creeping back in the middle of the night as I am missing you.

The talks we had, the laughs and love we shared and the life we faced together.

It wasn't perfect, but it always seemed to work for us in its own special way.

So, as a solitary tear rolls down my cheek and I try not to burst into tears, I force a smile through the storms of my discontent.

Those are the times I cling to – the happiness that we had – and somehow, it gets me through.

It may never be truly enough, but it helps me survive the hard moments ... when do you ever get enough of the right kind of love?

I curl into a ball and close my eyes, remembering that this too, shall pass.

Sleep overwhelms me as a solitary but wonderful thought sweeps over me:

For a time, it was us, it was beautiful and it was love.

Once in a While, Love Gives Us a Fairy Tale

In the fairy tales, it always goes the same:
Princess saved by the knight in shining armor
… they find white picket fences and a cozy
cottage and live happily ever after.
All my life, that's how I thought it was supposed
to be.
That's just how I imagined true love stories
happened.
I tried to save those who would not be saved
and ended up with nothing but heartache.
I chased others that weren't worth catching and
tried to love those who would not be loved.
I spent nights dreaming of my love
and days hoping with always the same result:
loneliness.
I'd hold onto that desire and close my eyes
whenever the chance arose … crossing my
fingers that love would come calling.
It was never meant to be … until I found the
right one.
Around every corner, I'd hold my breath,
Hoping a wonderful smile would greet me just
beyond.

Maybe, just maybe, the love of my dreams just wasn't real, that I wasn't meant to be part of a "we." Always the same result.

Always empty wishes and dead end hopes.

Days turn to months and months dragged into a blur.

I tried not to give up hope.

I wanted to believe that there's someone out there for all of us, including me.

I fought to believe that dreams come true and that my hopes would not be in vain.

Despair slowly crept into my days and angst deeper into my nights.

My wish had expired, it had seemed, and the light of my once promising dreams of love was fading.

Until one summer day, my head buried in my music, melancholy permeating my mind until suddenly, someone shook me out of my musical trance.

Opening my eyes, I discovered an amazing smile staring back at me.

She pulled the earphone from my ear, introduced herself and remarked that she couldn't help but overhear my music ...

She wondered why I seemed sad, because I

had a kind face.

Losing myself in those rueful hazel eyes, an epiphany sparked.

I had it wrong all along.

Maybe it wasn't always about the knight in shining armor saving the princess.

Maybe, just maybe, sometimes it's an amazing princess rescuing a wayward knight.

As we talked and walked, something inside of me changed.

It wasn't about who needed saving or being something I wasn't, it was about accepting whatever version of my love story showed up.

As I looked over at her beaming smile, I knew that the rules didn't matter and the details weren't important.

Two people, one soul, a beautiful ending to the happiest story that I could have imagined.

I didn't know how to write the opening chapters of my life, but now, I know how the story ends.

Life has a funny way of showing you a different way of thinking you never expected.

It all started with a smile … and ended with forever.

Once in a while, in the middle of an ordinary life, love gives us a fairy tale.

An Old Soul Caught Between a Strong Mind and a Fragile Heart

She was someone that most people just didn't understand ... not for their lack of trying.
She was always kind and smiling, but she never really let her guard down.
Her eyes spoke volumes about who she truly was, but most never bothered to look past her walls to uncover her depths.
Truthfully, she protected who she was with ferocity, saving her real beauty for her special ones ... the people who knew her on a different level, an intimate level ...
The people she loved were much like her – old souls with empathetic spirits that could read others in ways that intimidated some.
They possessed a wisdom beyond their years and a love deeper than the worldly version of superficiality.
Like them, she needed more than shallow love and mediocre passion.
If she couldn't give her all to someone or something, she walked away – she didn't know how to do anything halfway – including love.
She knew she wasn't for everyone, as there

would always be the people who wanted to love her but didn't know how.

Those were the ones that tried to love her on their terms without truly trying to unravel her mystery and engage her mind.

That was normal, she supposed, so she thought nothing of it.

The world was full of ordinary people leading nice lives with average dreams ...

She vowed never to walk that path ... it just wasn't for her.

Her soul yearned for the most intimate relationships and the contentment of deep love – both for herself and others – and she relentlessly pursued the happiness in what mattered most to her.

She didn't try to be different, she just was.

Her soul was distinctively rich and her mind was wired uniquely.

Honestly, she couldn't tell you why she was so soulfully passionate, only that her heart and soul wouldn't let her be any other way.

She shied away from the spotlight and reveled in the brilliant allure of the stars ...

But you'd often find her soaking in a beautiful sunrise or losing herself in the dying rays of a hued sunset.

She knew who she was, even if she couldn't really explain it sometimes.

She was an old soul, caught between a strong mind and a fragile heart ...

And most of all, she was beautiful,

She was unforgettable and

She was truly happy ... just the way she was.

My Heart is a Fiery Blaze

You want to win my heart, but do you really want to understand who and what I am?
I'm not everyone's cup of tea, and I'm much more than a shot of expresso ...
I don't live within labels and definitions – my heart and my soul are limitless in ways most people fear.
I love hard when there's love to be had, and I don't sacrifice who I am or what I want to be happy.
I expect what I give and I never settle.
Respect, loyalty, passion and courage ...
These aren't catch phrases to me, they're part of a code I live by.
True, I'm not for everyone, but then, I don't have to be.
All I want is my one.
My person who gets me when no one else does, who can read my soul through my eyes and speaks my language without saying a word.
I don't expect much, really ... or at least that's what I tell myself sometimes.
Yes, maybe my version of happily ever after is

unique and one of a kind, but so is what I
deserve.

I don't need someone to fix me, complete me
or make me happy.

I do want someone to stand beside me in the
storm, hold my hand in the dark and love me
on the days when I don't even like myself.

I understand that I'm a handful with a fiery
spirit, strong mind and deep soul, but I've built
who I am by walking through the fire of
brokenness.

So, if you think you have what it takes to dance
in the rain and love me like a hurricane, then
step up and let's see where our hearts take us.

I don't have all the answers – in fact, I don't
even know many of the questions – but I do
know this …

Once you've felt the ferocity of my love,
nothing else will ever do.

She Had This Weird Habit of Being Herself All the Time

It's always easiest to follow the crowd and do what everyone else is doing ...
But that's not what makes me happy, so I'll choose a different path.
I can't be what I'm not, and I'll never be just another copy duplicating what the rest are doing.
For some, that makes them happy.
For me, I need so much more than to lead an uninspired life.
I need the things that fill my soul and electrify my heart.
I'll always be the one who walks, talks and thinks like an original.
I wasn't meant to lead an ordinary life doing regular things –
And for some, they find happiness there ...
Not me.
I need more.
I need colorful sunsets and rainswept warm afternoons.
I want to be all the things that fulfill my spirit and ease my soul.

I crave adventure, pursuing out of the way places with my people finding our joy in the little things that get overlooked.

In a word, I just want to be happy.

I'll never be happy chasing someone else's dream or duplicating the efforts of others.

I know that sometimes I rub others the wrong way and not everyone is going to like me or the way I think ...

And I'm perfectly fine with that.

I'm not trying to change the world for everyone, I'm trying to change the world for one person: Me.

I'm not out to lead the crowd into being like me, I'm just listening to my heart and following my dreams.

I never said I was perfect or that my days were easy –

Only that I would tackle each and every challenge with an unbreakable spirit and a passionate attitude.

I'm not the strongest person I've ever met, but I'm strong in all the ways that matter to me.

I'm a loyal friend, a kind person and a devoted partner.

I strive to embody all the ideals I admire and

appreciate about the special people in my life.
I've learned along my journey that I don't have
to be the best to be happy ...
I just need happiness on my own terms.
I make mistakes and I conquer the mountains
that stand in my way, every day.
I may rise and I may fall, but I'll always do it my
way.
In the end, I'll be what matters most to me.
My own kind of unique and original happy.

The Person She Was Always Meant to Become

I've fallen to my knees so many times, never knowing how I'd rise again.

I lived my life saddled with too much of the negative emotions that weighed me down.

I didn't know how to let go of the shame, regret and sadness ...

I let all my bad choices and poor decisions of the past ruin my present and keep me from finding my joy.

Sometimes, when you're lost in the darkness, it's hard to find light – any light at all.

I thought it would be easier to simply dwell in the misery than to dig my way out ...

Turns out, that's the worst pain of all.

It's said that true strength is holding on, but I've found that is a different sort of strong.

Finding the courage to let go of the things that weighed me down was the hardest choice I've ever made ...

But that was the only real option I ever had.

Lingering in the past lamenting my countless broken hearts, wallowing in the pain I've caused others and regretting the bad choices

I've made began to taint my soul with darkness,
And that's not who I am or ever will be.
I may have nights of inexplicable sadness and days of unbelievable struggle, but I'd never change a thing about my journey.
It's made me who I am and forged my strength in ways that an easy life never could.
It's hard, almost impossible sometimes, but walking through the fire builds a foundation that sunlight and rainbows never will.
Give me the challenges and failures – I'll turn them into comebacks and a success story.
I lost my way many times trying to search for the light to lead me out of sorrow, but then I remembered – I was better than that.
That's when my soul led the way where my eyes had only failed me before.
My wings may have been clipped, but they're growing back stronger than ever.
My claws may have been dulled, but they're sharpening again.
My heart may have been broken, but it still beats with the ferocity of a hurricane.
I will never be perfect nor have days without sadness, but I know that I can overcome

anything with passion in my soul and love in my heart.

I'm finally finding the courage to let go of the painful past – and the truth will set you free.

Today, I'm starting a new chapter.

It's filled with disaster, heartbreak and raw emotions, but most of all,

It will always end with triumph, happiness and something that no one can ever take from me:

Sunlight in my soul, for now and always.

That light you see behind my eyes now … it wasn't found, it was forged.

The flames of the fire did more than test me, they gave me the strength to rise again from the ashes …

Reborn.

Stand Under the Stars with Me Forever

I don't need fancy promises of grandiose things
or expensive possessions.
Material gifts and tangible trappings are quite
nice – don't get me wrong –
but they're not what fuels our dreams and
gives life to our hopes ...
Certainly not what enriches true love ...
Our love.
Promises to visit faraway lands and the best
that money can buy will never be what I want
from you.
All that I want, for now and always, is just you.
The best things in life are and always will be
free ... your love, greatest of all.
Your best days, your worst times and all the
other ones squeezed in the middle –
facing them all by my side.
Kisses in the rain, hands held in the still of
night are what makes my heart beat wildly for
you.
The feeling of contentment of heart and soul
will always make me sigh when we touch.
The look in your eye that draws me in and the
smile that melts my heart –

that's why I will walk beside you until we can walk no more.
Our victories and our defeats,
tragedies and triumphs ...
It only makes our love that much more beautiful.
Our small memories and our grand accomplishments spark my spirit in ways I've never known.
Even the stormiest days followed by the brightest nights ...
These are all I want with you, side by side, taking on the world.
I don't need promises of things to make me happy.
It's pretty simple, really.
I just need you.
There's nothing else I could ever want ...
especially when I'm holding everything in my arms when I'm pulling you to me.
Falling asleep beside you is the waking dream I've waited a lifetime for ... and I would wait countless more if I had to.
It was always you and it always will be ...
You complete me in a way I never thought possible.

You and I have something special ...
Our happily ever after written in a style
distinctly our own.
There's no place I'd rather be than in your
arms, totally in love with you.
Forever and always, that's where I'll be.
Waiting for you, on the steps to love
forevermore.

Live Wild, Laugh Often, Love Hard

When she heard "you can't" and "you'll never,"
She would smile at their small mindedness.
They tried to define her by their terms with only
the limiting words they understood.
Never realizing that she was forged from a
different fire,
flames that seared her soul and scorched her
heart.
She knew what they told her was wrong,
because they had no idea who she truly was.
Truth is, they didn't really care, because to
them, she was unique … and being different
was scary to those who didn't understand her.
And she was different, in all the ways that
mattered:
Courageous, strong and free, she chased her
dreams and listened to her heart every day ...
in every way.
She looked for the joy in her days and let
laughter permeate her soul.
She loved with the ferocity of a wildfire –
nothing halfway or lukewarm in her desire ...
ever.
She wasn't just unusual or unique, she was

memorable in the way that a beautiful storm takes your breath away.

She was gorgeous in the way that a untamed spirit was wild and free ...

There wasn't a cage strong enough to hold her, Much to the dismay of the many who had tried to tame her and impose their will upon hers.

They didn't realize that a strong woman was most beautiful when she was loved on her terms and allowed to fly high and strong.

She wasn't one in a million or once in a lifetime, she was the only one of her kind ... ever.

She'd love you like a hurricane, overwhelm you like the strongest fire and seduce your senses like a mysterious siren.

She wasn't one of the women that tried to be original, she just ... was one of a kind.

She didn't apologize for who she was and never lived with regret.

Born with a soulful heart,

She loved with a fiery passion,

Lived with reckless abandon and always Dreamed with an unquenchable thirst.

She left her mark wherever she went and on the lives she touched along the way.

Her reasons for being who she was were the
sort that were interwoven into her soul,
the kind that moved her in ways that others
often didn't understand ...
But then, she didn't expect them to.
When you come across a creature awakened,
wild and free, sometimes you just have to smile
and embrace her in all her alluring appeal and
mystery.
The ones that chose to turn away didn't get
her, so she just let them wonder ... because
they weren't her people.
She knew the truth that you'd soon discover:
You'd never tame her, cage her or clip her
wings.
You could only hope, for a time, to spend every
amazing moment soaking in her
unencumbered persona.
After all, when you find something rare and
wonderful, all you can really do is appreciate it.
In the end, she was who she was:
Hard to find,
Difficult to understand,
And always impossible to forget.
Undeniably and unbelievably ...
She would always be wild, free and beautiful.

… And I Never Looked Back

Give me the beautiful souls that march to their
own beat,
The people that don't care about fitting in.
I want to surround myself with the ones who
aren't afraid to chase adventure and
experience life to the fullest.
I've had enough of ordinary living and simply
existing.
I want the things that are off the beaten path
and the feelings that escape definition.
Show me the way to the beautiful sunrises, the
warm breezes and the last hues of a dying sun.
It's time to start living in the moment and
breathing in the sweet air of happiness.
Fill my heart with passion and give me the
people who know how to truly live.
Forget doing what I've always done, I need to
enjoy the hidden beauty of life:
Sweet puppy kisses, the warm hugs of a dear
friend, the gleeful smile of a little child.
I want to feel and do all the things everyone
else is too afraid to uncover.
I yearn to fall in love with being alive every day,
and I want to taste the sweet joy of finding

purpose in whatever I pursue.

It's time to stop asking why I haven't and started asking how I can.

Dancing with my person in the rain, daytime trips to nowhere for no reason, laughter about nothing in the quiet of the night.

Those are but a few of the things that fill my heart and enrich my soul.

I want to fall in love with being alive, each and every day ...

In my own unique way –

Unfettered and unapologetically,

I'm going to chase the stars and seek the sunlight.

I've had enough of the things that weigh me down and make me unhappy.

This is my time to spread my wings and fly.

Join me, and let's go find some adventure,

Dreams don't come with an expiration date,

So let's go chase forever on the horizon.

Your Wild, Unpredictable Heart Knows What Your Soul Needs

I'm done living my life wondering why I haven't done more.
I'm going to do more than eat the cake, buy the shoes and take the trip ...
That's just day one.
No, I'm going to start filling my soul with the passion of living my purpose.
Forget ordinary dreams and average living.
I want more – I deserve more – I can be more.
I don't want to be a light or a candle in the wind, I choose to be on fire for life.
I am stepping out of my comfort zone as often as I can –
Redefining who and what I can be whenever the opportunity presents itself.
I need to seek the adventures that will make my heart smile and my spirit content.
Life is short, and while everyone else is worrying about what outfit they're going to wear,
I'm going to figure out whose life I'm going to change ...
Starting with my own.

Dreams are just desires without deadlines, so I'm going to chase them with all of my heart, mind and soul.

If I can't put my heart into it, I'll take myself out of it.

I may never change the world, but I can change it for one person:

Me.

After all, isn't that the one that matters most?

Rise and shine, I'm going to burn brightly,

My way.

Be Bold, Be Wild, Be Strong

I used to listen to all the people telling me what
I should and shouldn't be ...
And truthfully, it was exhausting.
What to wear, not to wear, what to say or do ...
I got to a point where I lost who I was in trying
to make everyone else happy.
That's when a beautiful friend told me to let go
of all the things I wasn't and start becoming all
the things I am meant to be.
I was perplexed, confused ... and relieved.
I couldn't be what everyone thought I should be
and simply be happy.
That's not real, and I'm not settling for
everyone else's opinion of my happiness.
No, I'm better than that, and I'm meant for so
much more.
Anyone can be beautiful, you know?
Your hairstyle, your clothes, your outward
appearance ... sure, those are attractive ...
But not in the ways that truly matter.
I'm leaving all that superficial shallowness
behind because I want more for myself, more
for my life.
Why settle for being just like everyone else?

I'm not.

I'm stepping out of the labels and expectations, and I'm blazing my own trail.

I will be beautiful in the most amazing ways that will rock a world full of fake.

I'm going to be bold, strong and confident each and every day ...

In my words, in how I love and what I do.

Forget a life of merely existing.

I want to be on fire for life, love and the people I care about.

They'll tell you not to have an attitude, be opinionated or different ...

So that's exactly what I plan to be:

Independent, fiery and original.

I'm going to ride the wind and chase my dreams with a style I'm happy to call my own.

I'm not borrowing, stealing or copying anyone else.

That's for the weak people who don't think for themselves.

I want to look in the mirror each and every day and know that I'm living life to the fullest –

Fiercely passionate and lovingly confident.

I'm going to do what all the others tell me that I can't do ...

I'll be brave enough to be real in a world full of copies.

I'm going to redefine beauty with a courage all my own.

My life, my voice, my way.

I'm never again going to allow myself to run with the rest when I'm destined to fly high.

I don't need a spotlight, my dear ...

I'll always shine from within.

Beautiful Things Have Dents & Scratches Too

I know I'll never be perfect, and I stopped trying to be a long time ago.
Once upon a time I tried to be everything for everyone, and it nearly destroyed me.
Now, I own who I am and let my light shine, regardless of what anyone thinks about it.
Life's too short to not be exactly what I want, how I want in the way I want.
All my life I was told what I can't do and why I can't do it.
The world told me I was too broken to ever be happy or find my way.
Well, the world was wrong.
This is my time, and I'm giving everyone a wake-up call.
I'm strong enough,
I'm good enough,
And I'll be beautiful enough ...
To do anything I set my mind to.
Yes, I've been broken in ways most could never imagine, and I've been down the wrong road too often.
But until you've walked through the fire, you

don't know just how strong you are.

Forget what they think they know about me.

I'm beautifully broken.

I didn't just face the fire ... I became it.

No one knows the path you've taken to become who you are unless they've been burned themselves ...

So, I don't care what anyone says about who I am or what I can do.

I'm an absolute mess some days with out of control hair and mismatched socks, but that will never define me –

It just adds to my impossible charm.

I'm one of a kind, strong and soulful, and I'll never accept anything less than the best ...

From the people in my life, the dreams I'm chasing and the love I deserve.

I'm never settling, making do or being okay with being an option.

So, if you're going to love me for me, accept me for all my scratches, dents and flaws, then take my hand ...

Let's go find the kind of adventures that fill our souls with love and set our hearts on fire.

All those people who thought they knew me and said I'd never make it …

They thought that because the world bruised my spirit,
That I'd let anything keep me from soaring high.
They were wrong.
Yes, my wings were broken for a time ...
But I was still able to fight my way back and reforge my fire ...
Because I didn't need my wings to survive ...
I still had claws.
Now it's my time to fly and shine.

Look for Someone Who Won't Let You Face the World Alone

When life brings you to your knees,
And you don't know where my turn,
As your hope fades like the last sunlight,
Know that I'll always be there for you.

I can't solve your problems
Nor do I have all the answers,
But I'm here to stand beside you
And always listen when you need it most.

There will always be storms,
And the times that threaten to tear us apart,
But hand in hand, side by side,
We can weather anything with love in our
hearts.

I'll be the first to embrace you after a long day,
Welcoming you home to my loving arms,
Kissing your forehead and stroking your hair,
Telling you it's all going to be okay.

Since we've met, we've never been apart,
For your heart is my home,

Your love is my refuge from life,
Our hidden haven from the world around.

Two hearts that found each other
When we needed it most.
Brought together for the most intimate reason,
For a true love like ours will
Always find its way.

We Fall in Love by Chance, We Stay in Love by Choice

Darlin',
When I fell in love with you,
I didn't know anything could feel this wonderful
... every time I get lost in your eyes,
I know how incomplete I was before I met you.
I never realized how amazing love could truly
feel ...
How one person could elicit such intense
passion while soothing my spirit at the same
time.
That was a feeling I never could have imagined
until you made it real.
But now that I do, I'll be planning to spend the
rest of my life choosing each and every day ...
To fall in love with you, all over again ...
Two hearts entwined, wrapped in love's
embrace until time is no more.
From the first glance I ever saw you until the
horizon meets the sky,
We will always be my favorite love story.

You Ask for a Match, I'll Give You a Wildfire

I know you're used to a different kind of love than you've found in me.
I realize that you don't know how to handle me and my intense passion ...
But the good news is, you don't have to ...
I wasn't meant to be "handled."
I'm here to be loved and to love, on equal terms and unconditionally.
Most of the time, you don't know what to make of my fiery demeanor and passionate spirit, and that's okay ...
You'll figure it out if I'm worth it ... and I know that I am.
I'm not a person who can love small or who does things halfway.
When I know what I want or like, I'm all in.
So, if I tell you that I love you, understand that I'm not asking permission or wanting approval ...
I'm just stating the facts and preparing you for my fierce but loyal heart.
I'm not like all the others, and I won't chase you,

I won't beg for your attention and hope to win some of your time.

After all, who would ever look past a roaring fire?

I know what I want and where I'm headed, and I hope you're up to the task.

I'll never be meek, quiet or faint of heart, so if you need someone who will accept being unequal, that's not me.

If you want the most out of life and love, then take my hand.

Every day is an adventure, and never in a straight line.

But that's the beauty of life, isn't it?

Unexpected diversions can turn into wonderful destinations.

Rain or shine, we will always end up where we are meant to be ...

With the wind at our backs and our faces to the sunlight,

There's nothing we can't do.

Forget lackluster love and mediocre passion ...

Let's immerse ourselves into each other and life ...

One beautiful moment at a time.

She Lies in the Darkness Overwhelmed

She lies in the dark,
Wishing she could turn off her mind.
Her thoughts never stop, and her emotions
threaten to overwhelm her.
She overthinks everything – there's no way to
change how she's wired.
No matter how amazing or terrible
something may be, she will analyze and
contemplate everything about it until she has
no peace about anything.
She doesn't want to be the way she is, letting
her mind constantly worry her, but it's just who
she is.
She worries about everything, because she
loves her people fiercely.
She wants the best for everyone in her life, and
she constantly turns things over in her head.
She doesn't have the answers for everything –
in fact, rarely so – but she is always
contemplating so very much ...
From what she has to do the next day, to the
next birthday she has to plan, or even the
smallest things like wondering if she should
replace the hand towels ...

She just lies there, stares at the ceiling … and thinks.

The house is quiet but her thoughts never are.

She struggles to sleep though her body is weary, but her mind keeps her vigilant –

Even when she knows she must sleep.

She looks forward to the moments when she finally gets drowsy and, for a time, sleep claims her,

calming her thoughts and refreshing her body.

As she drifts off into slumber, her soul smiles because she knows ...

She is blessed, loved and things always seem to work out ...

No matter how much she stresses about them, not that she will think less about anything.

That is who she is and how she cares, lives and loves ...

But she wouldn't change for anything ...

Though she might enjoy a bit more sleep at times.

She is and always will be the most beautiful of us all ...

Her … and her wonderfully tireless mind.

Becoming the Storm

I only wanted to be happy, that's all I set out to find. I didn't have a plan other than to listen to my heart and chase my dreams.
And while I didn't end up where I planned to go, I did arrive exactly where I needed to be.
I didn't choose to be strong … that never even crossed my mind.
Sometimes, you find your strength when being strong is your only option.
I stumbled and fell flat on my face so many times I wondered often if I should even keep getting back up.
But that's just who I am – I have fire in my veins and embers in my heart and I always will.
I don't know how to quit, and I'll never stay down for long.
I don't care what brings me to my knees, I will always stand back up and keep moving forward.
Truth is, I have been broken more often than I care to admit, but that was exactly what I needed to let the light into my soul.
My true strength isn't in how I kept from breaking, but rather in how I kept going after I

broke.

I don't have the answers and, most times,
I'm a beautiful disaster who is lucky to match
socks or remember what day it is.

The most wonderful part?

I don't have to have it all together, because I
never truly will ...

I like to say that's part of my charm.

So, for anyone looking for perfect, then don't
look to me.

I'm beautifully broken, but amazingly awesome
and always genuinely authentic.

And, oh yes, I'm also impossibly strong.

So, if you're looking for me,

You'll find me out dancing in the rain and
embracing the hurricane.

I may not be everything you've ever hoped for,
but I'll always be real, authentic and true ... and
maybe exactly what you never knew you
always needed. Mind, spirit and soul,

I'm strong in all the ways that matter.

So now, every time life tries to bring me to my
knees, looks me in the eye and tells me
"You can't withstand the storm,"

I simply smile back and say
"I am the storm."

Life Needs More Slow Dances, Stolen Kisses and Quiet Moments

My love,
Let's stop time for a bit and lose ourselves in
the moments –
Our frozen cocoon of love that will melt the
world away as we simply enjoy our love story
for a long and wonderful rendezvous.
Let's slow dance wherever we are,
Let's slow kiss whenever we can,
And let's just slow down and love each other
as often as we should.
Let's never let life stop us from stealing away
from the world and reclaiming our passionate
love.
This is the magic that will keep us falling in love
every day.
Kiss me deeply like every time is the first time
... The last thought as I fall asleep each night
and the first smile as I rise each morning,
That is my wish and promise to you,
For always.
Let's do more than just love each other
respectfully, devotedly and passionately ...
Let's promise to always carve out the moments

that we will transform into beautiful memories
... Slow dances in the kitchen,
Stolen kisses in a hidden doorway,
Quiet moments of love that we will treasure
throughout our years together.
Let's stoke the fires of our love,
One beautiful moment at a time ...
Forever in your arms,
until all fades away into love's embrace,
Evermore.

Be a Child Again ... Act Silly, Chase a Butterfly ... Find the Wonder

I needed more than just a break, I craved a new direction.
I took a deep breath and closed my eyes, shutting out the world for just a moment.
I put aside all the pressures and thought back to when I was small ...
When everything was new and the possibilities were limitless.
Life was full of wonder and my dreams were still very real and vibrant.
I believed that I could and would do whatever I set out to accomplish.
Opening my eyes, I smiled as I realized that sometimes, the hardest answers are the easiest to find.
It was time for me to remember who I once was and the dreams I had as a child.
It's time for me to rediscover that magic that I had lost along the way and breathe life into my spirit again.
I want to laugh and giggle for no reason and dream for every reason.
I want to be silly and have the adventures that I

once loved.

I'm going to dip my cookies in milk, and I'm no longer okay with accepting negativity in my life.

I want to let the puppies lick my face, and I'm going to chase the butterflies ...

I'm going to remember what it means to truly be alive again.

I'm going to fill my soul with the childlike glee of happiness, starting with today.

I know it won't change my life, but it will change my perception ... which can change my trajectory.

I'm taking back my power and finding my magic, because I deserve to be happy.

I'm going to see all the little things that once escaped me, and I'm going to celebrate the joy of being alive every day.

The serene beauty of a starlit sky, the soothing calm of a peaceful wind – all the things that surround us will help me find my contentment.

I know that life will still have its challenges and the troubles of today will still be there,

But I will no longer allow those things to control my emotions and affect how I feel.

It's a new day and a new chapter ... and I'm finding my joy again.

I'm going to dance in the rain and chase the rainbows.

This is my life, and I'm choosing to love harder, laugh deeper and become more.

With love in my heart, a childlike spirit and passion in my soul, I can do anything ...

Starting with writing the newest chapter of my life.

I call it ...

Finding my magic again.

When You Are Happy with Who You Are, It Won't Matter Who Isn't

I realized a long time ago that we all shine differently in unique ways.
You and I may see things differently, but it doesn't mean that either of us is wrong.
Our individual journeys to happiness are as different as we are, as well they should be.
I had to find my way to my true self, and honestly,
It was the hardest thing I've ever had to do.
I had all the questions and none of the answers
... And I had no idea where to start looking for my path.
When you've been mired in the darkness for so long, finding the light isn't as easy as you might think.
But, with the people who held my hand along the way, trusting the magic of new beginnings and just believing in myself, I found my way.
I stumbled,
I fell,
And I cried myself to sleep so many nights,
Not wanting to be lost anymore.
But you see, sometimes you have to lose

everything you are to discover who you might
become and where you're meant to be.
Some said I'd never find the answers I was
looking for and there was no way I could ever
truly be happy with myself.
I've never been more happy to prove anyone
wrong ... and prove myself right.
That I could do it, that I was strong enough
and, most of all, that I was good enough.
It wasn't easy, it wasn't fast, but it was worth it
for so many reasons I'll always be thankful for.
So, if you're lost and don't know how to find the
your way anymore,
Take my hand and let's go find some
happiness.
There's a beautiful place waiting just for us,
In that place past the pain and hurt.
I know who I am and most of all, I'm happy with
the person I've become.
The best part of all?
I don't care who disagrees with me –
It's my life and my journey.
They don't know where I've been
Or where I'm going, and I'm good with that.
I'm just one of those people ...
Always meant to spread my wings and fly high.

You Don't Deserve Someone Who Comes Back, You Deserve Someone Who Never Leaves

What hurt me most isn't that we fought and you said hurtful things.
I'm thick skinned and I can get past words …
though remember that words can cut the deepest.
What breaks my heart is that instead of fighting for us and working with me to find a way through our problems,
You chose to walk away and turn your back on me.
You took the easy way out, and now that you've decided you're ready to come back,
You think that I should be welcoming you with open arms?
Truth is, I can't just bury the pain between us and the hurt you caused when you ran.
You think I should be grateful you came back?
Think again, my dear.
I may have been broken, and I may not always know the right answers, but I do know this:
I know who I am and what I'm worth …
More than that, I know what I deserve.

You've always seemed to think that you know what's best for me, but you proved otherwise when you hurt me by leaving so quickly.

I don't need to be rescued or fixed, and I don't need anyone to make me happy ...

There's a big difference between want and need,

And what I need most in a partner is courage – someone who won't walk out on me when things get hard ...

A partner who will be a rock through the storms when we need it most.

I used to think that was you, and

I'm sad now that I've realized it's not.

Thank you for loving me in your way and for helping me to understand what I truly deserve in life and love ...

And it's not someone who can't handle the hard stuff, a partner who+ quits when the going gets tough.

I'll never need anyone to be happy with myself, so I've decided next time,

I'm not settling for just anyone to love me,

I'm holding out for a hero.

Because that's who I am and exactly what I deserve.

It doesn't take heroism to believe in love,
But it does take someone who will do the one
thing you couldn't ...
fight for us, each and every day.

Keep the Ones Who Heard You When You Never Said a Word

They're the ones that always just get me – my
friends, my circle ...
The people who are always there when I need
them most – the ones I call before any others.
We may not talk for weeks or even months, but
when we do, we don't miss a beat.
They are the ones holding my hand through
everything ...
Laughing 'til our sides hurt, sharing the tears
and celebrating the victories.
Those people, my tribe, they're in my corner no
matter what goes down and when ...
They never judge or condemn me – they just
love me unconditionally.
They're the keepers – the friends who fill my
heart with joy and encourage my dreams.
They've picked up my broken pieces when life
and love has shattered me, and they've loved
me through the storms, the rainbows and
everything else in between.
When I come to them, devastated and broken-
hearted, they're the ones who sit with me,
Hold my hand and just listen while they wipe

my tears away.

There's just something comforting about knowing that, come what may, I'll never have to face the triumphs and tragedy alone.

They can look at me and, without saying a word, know everything that is going on with me.

They are the family we choose, and I'll keep choosing them, every day in every way.

So, if you have those people like I do, hold onto them and never let them go.

Cherish the memories you make together and count your blessings every time you see each other.

Time is fleeting – don't let a day go by that you don't let them know you're thinking of them ...

We all need more love like that in our lives.

So, to all my loved ones out there who have danced with me in the rain, stood strong beside me through the storms and flown high with me chasing our dreams ...

Thank you for all that you are and what you will always mean to me – you're loved more than you know.

Life is ever the more beautiful when you share it with the ones you love.

They'll always be the people who know everything you're saying when you don't even speak a word.

How Long Has It Been Since Someone Looked Past Your Eyes and Captured Your Soul?

You've spent your life alone but longing,
Hoping someone would see past the smile,
Searching for your soul that lay hidden
Beneath your fiery countenance.

You've struggled down the wrong roads,
And survived the broken hearts,
Kissing all the wrong frogs,
Whilst waiting for your long lost love.

Always wanting, never knowing but hoping,
You believed that true love would come for
you.
You read all the stories and cried at all the
movies,
And you knew you were still incomplete.

You're tired of the shallow ones who
Seek superficial pleasures of desire,
When you have never been the person
Who will accept just one night.

You know your worth and it's greater
Than any of the wrong choices ever knew,
Their broken roads just led you precisely
Where you're supposed to be ... in my arms.

Our souls found each other and recognized
The love that we found in that moment.
I'll never change the past or where we've been,
Because we were always meant to be ...
Two hearts, one beat, for a lifetime …
evermore.

She's the Fire and He's Afraid of Being Burned

You knew from my first hello exactly what type of woman I was.
Strong, vivacious and vibrant, there was no mistaking the fire that burned inside me.
You really don't know what to do with my truth – I see it in your face and hear it in your voice.
You've never met a woman like me, so I get that – the unknown can be frightening.
You're torn between what you think you want and what you know you need.
It's true, I'm not for the faint of heart or the weak spirited ... And I don't plan on changing.
I don't accept maybe or possibly from anyone wanting more of my time, so this is your wake-up call.
Will you play it safe or will you dare to venture where you've never gone?
I'm not everyone's favorite flavor, but then some people like watered down coffee and flavorless food.
I make no apologies for who I am and what I deserve ... which, if you're wondering, is the best from everything and everyone.

I love with all my heart and live with all my passion, so I expect the same from my people. No halfway love or living without purpose will ever have a place in my life.

So, if you want to step up and step out of your comfort zone, then I'll gladly take your hand and chase our dreams together.

If you're unsure or hesitant, then I'm not the gal for you. I'm burning for life in all the ways that matter, and there's no lie in my fire.

You'll always know where you stand with me and I'm never afraid to speak my mind ...

That's actually part of my charm, in case you didn't know.

So, I'm offering you the chance to be a part of my life if you're up to taking risks and being fully alive.

Step up or step aside, I'm not waiting on anyone who doesn't value my time or know my worth.

Yes, I walked through the flames to become the woman that I am, and I wouldn't change that for anyone or anything.

The question is – are you afraid of being burned ...

Or do you think you can handle my fire?

He Gave Her the Ocean Because She Didn't Want the Moon

When you came into my life,
All you wanted was love and respect.
You didn't ask for fancy dinners and expensive gifts.
You needed someone to see you for who you truly are and always would be.
The others before me had never really understood the magic of your soul.
They looked past the things that mattered to find the things they wanted.
That wasn't love, it was selfish.
You'd never been appreciated and respected the way you deserved.
You'd been holding out for a hero and all you got was a narcissistic zero.
They didn't love you … they loved what they wanted you to be.
Love is unselfish, it is kind, it is compassionate and so many things that you've never found before.
So, you may not ask for the sun, moon and stars, and though you deserve so much more than that, let's start with something every day.

Falling in love.

Being kind and considerate.

Always being thoughtful and respectful.

Communicating and being there for each other, through the tragedies and triumphs.

I'll dance with you in the rain and I'll hold you tightly through the storms.

There's nothing I won't do for you – this I promise, for now and always.

You didn't want the stars or moon, so I'll bring you the ocean instead ...

For every night as the water rushes in to find the shore,

So shall my love always be.

True and without fail,

Know that I loved you before I ever knew you ... When you were just a thought and dream, you were always my love.

Sing to me the song of your heart, my love, and let's lose ourselves in the magic of our love story ...

For you are and always will be, my waking dream that finally came true.

Strong Women Fight with Grace in Their Hearts, Kindness in Their Voices and Love in Their Souls

She wasn't strong because she wanted to be, but because she didn't have any other choice. When she was at her lowest point, all she could see was the anguish around her heart ... All she felt was the pain from the broken promises and people who had walked away. Her soul was weary and her heart had gotten heavy, and she knew she had to dig her way out of the darkness.
She didn't know where she'd find a light or even which direction to head, only that she wouldn't give up until she found peace.
She was tired of being sad and broken hearted, weary of the people who tried to trample her heart for their own pleasure.
No more weakness, no more lies.
She vowed to surround herself with authentic people, the ones she could count on when she needed them most.
She'd rather have five close friends than countless fair weather people ...
Her life was too precious to spend any time

convincing other people to love her on her terms.

She knew her worth and wouldn't settle any more for the ones who didn't make her a priority.

Her kind voice and loving soul was but a sliver of the depth of her amazing person, one that she intended to lock away until someone could see past her pain ...

The one who could speak to her soul ...

The lost half of a broken circle that was her.

She didn't need to be fixed, completed or saved.

She just wanted to be loved, on equal terms with respect and passion for the remainder of her days.

Her wants weren't extravagant or demanding, but her standards were.

She loved fiercely and was loyal to a fault – she expected the same from her loved ones and partner.

She'd been down the broken road too many times to count, and perhaps she'd travel there some more, but she was done chasing love and affection.

A gentleman wouldn't expect her to chase him,

and more importantly, he wouldn't let her.
Come what may, she'd never be anyone's "maybe."
This time, she was holding out for forever.

You Will Attract Beautiful Things into Your Life Once You Accept That You Are Worthy

All my life people told me that I wasn't good
enough and that I got what I deserved.
I was judged by those who didn't know me and
made to feel like I wasn't worth anything.
They'd have me believe that I'd never be
happy and that I should accept the love of
whoever I was lucky enough to find.
They couldn't have been more wrong ...
they don't know me and definitely don't know
what I deserve.
That ends now.
I'm taking back my power and I'm changing my
path.
I know who I am and what I want and I'll accept
nothing less.
I am good enough, I am worth it and I do
deserve to be happy.
I'm standing up and letting my voice be heard,
telling the rest of them that I don't care what
they think.
They don't know my struggle – they don't know
where I've been or what I've overcome,

They don't get to define me or my worth.

I'm going to find the beautiful people who will love me unconditionally, the partner who will respect me unequivocally and the dreams that I will never let go of.

This is my time and my choice, and I choose to be more.

More than what everyone else said I could be, more than I've ever been before.

I may not have all the answers and I'll still stumble and fall, but I'll always do it by my own terms.

I've failed but I'm not a failure.

I've been broken, but I'm still beautiful.

I've been lost, but I'll find my way.

They scorned me because I was different, and I don't really care – now I'm celebrating my uniqueness.

I'm authentic, I'm real and I'll always speak my mind.

I'm not taking the easy road and I know that it'll be challenging, but nothing worth having comes without struggle.

I know I'll have to kiss a few frogs before I find my love, and I'm okay with that.

Once in a lifetime love won't just happen

without work and patience –
But I won't settle, I won't quit and I'll never
demand anything less than the best.
I'm worth all the love and so much more.
I'm more than "enough,"
I'm amazing.
Just watch me while I go and change the
world, one heart at a time ...
Starting with my own.

You Have Me

From worlds apart against impossible odds,
Your heart found mine as destiny wove its
magic,
Uniting our souls as was always meant to be,
The universe conspiring to create our love.

Unwavering, unbreakable and unending,
Our story transformed into a love
Unlike any we had ever known.
We had always believed against hope that we
would find each other ...

As I hold your hand and gaze into your eyes,
Know that you are my everything –
Soulmate, best friend and lover,
A safe place more amazing than I could have
imagined.

Until the last star in every galaxy burns out,
And the whisper of life breathes no more,
Know this one simple truth:
You have me –
now and forever … and you always have.

The Worst Kind of Pain Is Getting Hurt by the Person You Explained Your Pain To

What hurts the most as I think about hearing those painful words you said isn't what you said ...
But who said them.
When our love was young and new you told me you'd never forsake me.
You promised me that you'd never leave me and that you would stand beside me through any storm.
I'd been hurt so many times before, and though I didn't trust love,
You made me believe I could trust you enough to take my walls down.
That you'd not break my heart like the ones before.
I wanted to let you in to see the real me, to finally have someone who saw and loved me for me.
But in those few seconds when you turned your back on me,
everything that we had built – and once believed in – came crashing down.

I never thought you'd be the one to break my heart because you knew the journey I'd taken to mend my bleeding heart.

You knew how scared I was to love again, and still you decided to go instead of staying and trying to save us.

I can forgive you for so much, but never for leaving and giving up without fighting for love, for us.

There were no words that could comfort my ailing spirit and no light behind my eyes, for our once beautiful future had fallen into decay.

As I watched you walk away, I fought back the tears and struggled to keep it together.

Some people come into your life for a season, a reason or a lesson ...

You were all those things for me when I most needed to find a way to believe again.

In love, in hope ...

That maybe dreams can come true.

Yes, it hurt for a long time when you left – I may never truly get over you ...

But I know as more time passes, I will be grateful for you and what you taught me.

It doesn't mean it will be easy to accept or the memories won't be painful,

But I'll realize the truth of what you showed me.
It's okay to open your heart and believe in love
even when some people may not deserve or
appreciate that love.
It's up to us to figure out who truly is worth it.
While you weren't the one meant to be my
person, you did show me the way to a healthier
and happier me.
I guess I should thank you midst my tears for
setting me free.
Somewhere,
Someone else is looking for a love like mine.
That, for now, will be more than enough to
make me smile ...
And find a way to believe again.

You Did Something for Me I Couldn't Do for Myself. You Loved Me for Who I Am

There was a time when I didn't know how to love myself the way that I knew I should.
I believed all the worst things about myself and didn't know how to believe any of the best.
I knew that I would never truly be able love anyone else the way they deserved if I couldn't start with loving myself.
I didn't know where to start or when what to do, so I just threw myself into trying to believe I was good enough,
That I was truly worthy of love.
I frustratingly tried to fight and dig my way to a deeper understanding of who I am ...
Until you showed up in my life and showed me parts of me I didn't even know existed.
You were the light that illuminated the way to a better and brighter appreciation for who I am and showed me what I could be.
You made me want to evolve, each and every day – improving and evolving for the person who not only changed my life but my heart as well.
Thank you for so many things – but most of all,

thank you for loving me when I didn't even know how to love myself.
You are and will always be ...
My one true thing and the best thing that ever happened to me.
My love, my soulmate, my twin flame.
Because of you, I'm able to believe in me, you and our future.
You showed me how to love in the most beautiful way of all –
Through your eyes.

I May Always Miss You and Love You ... but That Doesn't Mean I'd Take You Back

I came across a picture of you the other day and I couldn't help but smile.
Not because seeing you made me happy, but because I will always have the memories ...
Some good, some bad ... all very real.
The times we had and the love we shared will always have a special place in my heart.
We fought for a love that just wasn't meant to be – but it doesn't change how I'll always feel about you.
You can love someone and know that they belong in your heart, not your life.
Truth is, I can't really remember why we didn't make it, and it doesn't matter now.
I won't think poorly of you or of us, because we had something beautiful for a time.
You loved me in your way and tried your best to always make me feel special ...
I'll forever appreciate that about you.
I learned so much about life and love from my time with you, and I wouldn't change a thing, even if I could.

Love sometimes isn't enough to carry two people past the emotional distress they face together.

You need more than that: respect, empathy, compassion and communication.

I'll never forget you and the magical kisses and frozen moments in time that will always have a special place in my heart.

A tiny part of me will forever miss you and wish we were together again, but I know things happen for a reason ...

I'm happier now for what happened and what I learned after we parted ways.

We were never meant to find our forever together, and though I cried endless tears many nights about losing you, I know now that I'm a better person because of what happened between us.

You forced me to look harder at the parts of myself that I tried to bury in our relationship – I can't thank you enough for helping me to understand the path to a happier and healthier me.

So, if I ever saw you somewhere across the way, I'd look at you and simply smile at the memories of what we once had.

For a time

It was real, it was beautiful and it was love.

But I'll always be glad you let me go ...

That's when I finally learned how to truly love myself.

There Is Nothing Stronger Than a Woman Who Has Rebuilt Herself

When people see her they see a warm smile and a gentle nature.

Most will never venture past her facade that protects who she truly is.

They'll never know her journey through the fire and the battle to reforge herself in the flames of struggle ...

And she's okay with that.

She's not a person who shares herself freely – the ones who truly get her are the people who looked past her eyes.

Her circle are the loved ones who embrace her for all of her flaws, scars and scratches.

They love and accept her for who she is, and she's a marvelous creature once you begin to fully grasp the layers of her depths.

She's always fierce in her loyalty and beautiful in her love, she's the one who's there when people need someone most.

She's rebuilt herself after she was knocked down countless times, and she'll never forget the failures that pushed her to find a way through the fire.

Her past will not define her and her future will never be limited by what others think she should do or be.

She's broken in the most beautiful ways, so that the light will always get in to illuminate her soul.

She celebrates her scars and remembers each bruise, because those are the lessons that taught her how to discover herself.

So, if you want to try to understood the true marvel of this woman,

Prepare to dive into her depths and explore the hidden beauty that lies within.

She's fragile like a firestorm and strong like a wildflower –

Never predictable and always passionate.

She'll love you like a hurricane and leave you always wanting more.

She'll never be "just a woman" …

She's unique and wonderfully deep ...

And if you only scratch her surface,

You'll understand that there's so much more to her than meets the eye.

She'll make sure you never forget it.

With a warrior heart and poetic soul, she's more than one of a kind,

She's a once in a lifetime woman.
You'll always remember when you met the
woman who changed your life,
If only for an instant.
You'll never forget that smile … and that
amazing strength.

I Stopped Shrinking Myself to Fit the People I've Outgrown

I decided to stop trying to be whatever everyone else thought I should be.
I learned a long time ago that not everyone would like me or understand me ...
And I'm good with that.
I don't have to dim someone else's light to make mine shine brighter.
I think big and dream bigger, so there are people who will always look down on me because I'm not like them.
Here's a spoiler: I like me just the way I am, and I'm not changing to make anyone else happy.
I'm done to trying to please everyone else because all that ever did was make me unhappy.
I'm leaving those small people with small minds and smaller ideas in my past:
I'm not letting anyone or anything keep me down.
Forget the boxes they tried to fit around me and the labels that never really worked,
I'm more than a size, a stereotype or a number

on the scale.

I've got a lot of love to give and a beautiful soul to share with the people I care about.

I keep my circle small and my heart guarded –
I'm not going back to those places that tore me down before.

I burned the bridges that led me to the wrong places with the wrong people long ago.

This is a new day and a new me:
I'm living with purpose and loving with passion.

The ones who love me will always be right beside me, cheering me on and sharing the light.

You can keep your lukewarm desire and your mediocre love,
I don't believe in doing anything halfway.

If you can't give me your respect, love and passion the way I deserve, then that's your choice.

I've got one life, and I'm not settling for anything less than the best in my dreams, my friends and most of all, my partner.

Some may say I've got an attitude, and they're right … it's strong.

I know what I want and who I am, and I'll accept nothing less than the very best from the people in my life.

So, if you want to try to define me by all the other people you've ever known, let me stop you right there.

You've never met anyone like me and you never will again.

So, if you want to love me on my terms with the respect and passion that I expect, then take my hand and let's chase some adventure.

If you think I'm like the others and that I fit into the smaller boxes of lesser people,

Try again.

You can't cage my strong spirit and fiery heart, so don't even try to dull my shine.

I've got dreams to catch and love to share, so if you can't handle my truth,

Perhaps you should look elsewhere.

It's my time to soar and spread my wings, and I'm excited about my future.

The question is, can you accept me just the way I am?

Can You Miss Someone That You've Never Even Met?

Looking at my phone I couldn't believe the feelings I was experiencing.
They're just words on a screen ...
A voice in my ear.
That can't be real … can it?
Can a person sight unseen,
Touch unknown and kiss untasted ...
Find their way so deeply into your soul,
Become so entwined throughout your heart,
That the most impossible and unfathomable emotions come crashing into your mind?
You can't explain it, and even if you wanted to, could you?
Those words … that voice … those feelings …
belong to a person you've never actually met, touched or felt?
How can one heart so far away melt away your walls and see your soul without ever having looked into your eyes?
Can you miss someone when you've never even known their presence?
A million times before and countless days in the past,

I'd have told you there wasn't a way.

Impossible.

Illogical.

Nonsensical.

But then you came along, and everything changed.

You challenged everything that I ever believed and made the noise all fade away.

Your heart found mine in the most improbable way.

No way became yes,

Impossible transformed into "of course,"

And your soul found mine.

When love finds its way and destiny comes calling … nothing else matters.

We don't choose who we love and how it happens … it chooses us.

Accept it and be happy.

That's what I'll do.

I'll love you, because that's just what makes me feel complete.

You've shown me that love is so much more than a touch, a look or a feeling.

It's something you feel deeply in your soul, and because of you,

I wouldn't have it any other way.

She Waits for the One Who Can Read Her Soul for the Depth That Lies Within

She's not a chapter or short story,
she's a full length novel waiting to be
unraveled.
She has layers of beauty that aren't visible to
the naked eye or casual bystander ...
Her charm and wit will disarm you long before
you ever discover her secrets or dare venture
into the depths of her soul.
Untamed and unfettered, she has the heart of
a wildfire and spirit of a warrior maiden.
She waits for the one who will see behind her
soulful eyes and past her smirking smile,
She longs for the love that she has waited
endless night for – the one to stand apart from
the others that she left behind.
She may not be your cup of tea, but she'll most
certainly be your shot of expresso.
Fiery and passionate, she'll stoke your desires
and engage your mind.
As she walks away leaving you breathless,
you'll realize exactly who what she is ...
Perhaps too late.
She's a wild spirit that cannot be tamed and a

force of nature that cannot be contained ...
If you try to catch her eye or win her heart, prepare to invest your time as well as your love.
Engage her mind, call to her soul, stoke her heart – if you have any hopes of catching this beautiful butterfly.
She's not a quick read nor is she easy to understand ... Every page of her novel is unlike any other you've ever experienced ...
Turn the pages slowly and take it all in, for you're about to behold the most beautiful sight you'll ever see:
The heart and soul of a woman.
And the deeper you read, the more you'll fall in love.
She's not a happily ever after,
she's a wonder to behold …
The type of adventure that redefines the limits of your passion.
Forget the fairy tales, she's a wildfire waiting to incinerate your heart.
It's a fiery penance that you'll enjoy ...
every moment as she scorches your soul.
She is and always will be more than "just" a woman ...

She's the rarest of wildflowers … strong, wild and free.
Most of all, she's utterly unforgettable in all the best ways.

Give Me All of the Awkward Beauty You Try to Hide. I Promise I'll Love It

I know your heart is scared and you don't think you're worthy of love sometimes.
Your heart has been broken and your walls are high, and I get that.
I've been where you are and I know exactly how you feel.
I can't promise you that letting down your walls will be easy –
Because it won't be.
I can't promise that you won't struggle with your journey back to trusting love.
I can't promise that you won't be scared.
But this is what I know:
I'm here ...
With love in my heart and patience in my spirit to hold your hand through the rainy days.
You were told you weren't good enough and made to believe you weren't worthy of love.
They couldn't have been more wrong.
What I see before me is a beautifully broken soul that has survived the pain of a hard road and emerged stronger and better.
Your heart is gorgeous and your soul is

amazing.

Sure, we all have days when our socks don't match and our hair won't cooperate, but that just makes me adore you that much more.

What you think of as your awkwardness, I see as the unique quirks that set you apart.

Forget what you've been told or how the past made you feel, because it was all wrong.

You're a stunning one of a kind person who I wouldn't change a thing about, and you make my heart smile in ways I've never known.

So keep walking with your distinct style, because that's the person who I fell madly in love with.

Heart, mind, body and soul,

You'll always be beautiful in my eyes.

Fire in My Heart, Courage in My Spirit and Love in My Soul

Give me the moments that will inspire my life with amazing memories.
I want the indescribable times that fill my soul:
Blustery wind blowing through my hair on a winding road,
The beauty of a star-filled sky that shines brightly,
The wonder of a brilliant sunrise that breathes life into my spirit.
I want to experience all of the things that move me to greatness.
I need the moments of happiness that enrich my heart.
The hug of a long-missed friend that welcomes me home.
The laughter of a child that makes my soul smile.
The hope that every tomorrow I can bring joy to someone else.
I don't want to dream in black and white, but in all the colors of a life well lived.
Give me the adventures that will fill my days with amazement and contentment,

Having chased my dreams with relentless
desire and fulfilled my passions without regret.
I may not know what tomorrow brings, but with
fire in my heart,
Courage in my spirit, and love in my soul,
I'll enjoy every moment of my days ...
Sunrise to sunset,
Dawn to dusk and all the beauty in between.
I'll always find my path to the light ...
For now and always,
That's just who I'll be.
I couldn't ask for anything more.
My life, my way.

I'm Bruised but Not Broken. I'm Flawed but Not a Failure. I'm Beautiful Just the Way I Am.

I've spent most of my life trying to figure out who I am, what I want or where I belong.

Everyone told me all the things I should be and tried to make me fit inside the box of what was acceptable.

Everyone had an opinion of who I should be and why I should be like them.

The thing is, none of those definitions of me ever truly made me happy or captured who I was.

Sometimes, to discover the answers to the hardest questions, you've got to step outside your comfort zone and search your soul.

I had to stop listening to everyone else's opinions and start hearing my own heart and soul.

Turns out, most of the answers I needed I already knew, hidden in the places of me that I ever knew to look in.

The world will try to conform you to what it wants, and it's never really about who you should be.

I'm tired of the labels and I'm no longer going to march to anyone else's beat.

Only I know what makes me happy and what I seek in this life.

I want the things everyone wants, but I want more.

More than happiness, I want to be on fire for life and the things that bring me joy.

More than comfort, I want to go to the places that challenge me to become more,

To evolve into a better version of me.

More than love, I want to be engorged with white hot passion and intense desire for soulful fulfillment.

My road has been hard and the challenges many.

I've fallen and stumbled, but I never stayed down.

My heart has been battered, but it still beats vigorously.

I learned from my failures and became better from my disappointments.

I never wallowed in my setbacks and I always kept my face to the sunlight.

I'm one of a kind, once in a lifetime and truly gorgeous in the ways that matter.

Most of all, I'm always going to be
unapologetically me.
I'm broken, I'm beautiful and I'm always going
to find my way.
If you want to find me, look to the horizon ...
Chasing dreams and lassoing the stars.
I've got one chance at this life,
And I'm always going to give it my all.

Tonight I'll Dream You Are Here

You've been gone so long,
I wonder sometimes if you were ever truly real.
The times we had, the love we shared, the
memories we made ...
All seems to dissipate into nothingness as I try
to think back to us and what we had.
Your smile, your laughter, I think back to when
I was in your arms and those moments I
wanted to never end.
We swore to each other that we were meant to
be and that our love was forever.
It turns out that sometimes, love alone isn't
enough.
It makes me smile ... and cry.
I miss you so much it hurts, and I wish I knew
all the answers to why you're not in my life.
I hope that I'll see you again and that we will
find our way, but right now, I'm a mess.
I fight back the tears when our song plays and
smile when someone asks about you.
All I can do is hope and wonder.
What we had was love, it was real and it was
powerful.
I try to hold those precious droplets of joy in my

heart and wish for time to heal our wounds.

I wouldn't trade any time with you for the rest of my days –

You were the first to love me in a way I had never known ...

You loved me for me.

I don't know what tomorrow will bring, but I do know that I'll see you tonight ...

In my dreams.

At least there, I'll be forever happy.

Until then, I make wishes and keep hoping.

The sun always rises.

Even in my dreams.

… until I Finally Started to Love Me for Me

I'd always heard all the talk about loving
yourself, but I never thought it applied to me.
I thought simply being happy was enough.
I'd presumed that loving someone else would
give me everything I needed.
Everything was fine … until they walked away
and left me holding my heart in my hands.
That's when I understood why loving others
without putting yourself first will never be
enough.
I had staked all my hopes and dreams on one
person, and truthfully, that wasn't fair to either
one of us.
Their goals became mine, and I thought I
enjoyed everything they did ...
But I was wrong.
It was their happiness that I enjoyed, because
that's how I love, unselfishly.
Putting them first and always wanting them to
be happy was just my way.
So, when heartbreak found me alone and
holding the shattered dreams of a love lost, I
didn't know how to make myself happy

anymore.

I certainly didn't know how to love myself – not in any way that mattered.

I had lost who I was and what I wanted along the way, and it's hard to put yourself back together again.

You listen to the advice, read the books and bury yourself in music, hoping the therapeutic effect will lead you to the path you're searching for.

It's not easy, it's not painless and there are a lot of restless thoughts and sleepless nights. Truthfully, I didn't realize how much I needed to love myself until I finally started to find my truth.

Seeking my joy and living in my moments became not just an option, but a necessity.

I understood for the first time that I could never truly love another until I loved myself first.

I did a lot of soul searching and endured many painful internal battles, but it was worth every tear and each hard revelation.

Learning to be comfortable with who you are is a journey that never really ends,

It just evolves as your path goes deeper.

I forgave myself for all the things I had never

really let go of before, and I marveled at how light my burdens became once I did.

In the end, my greatest love story became my own ...

Falling in love with myself will always be my most beautiful and favorite

happily ever after.

I Can't Promise to Fix All of Your Problems, but I Can Promise You Won't Have to Face Them All Alone

My love ...
My promise to you on this day,
As on all the days to come ...
I can't make the rain go away,
Nor make the sun to shine again ...

But I can be your shelter through any storm.
I'll never have all the answers,
Nor always know the right way,
But I'll be there to share the walk
and hold your hand through the rain.

I can't promise easy days,
Nor times without struggle,
But I will be there for you,
Facing the world by your side.

I can't fix your problems,
Nor make them disappear,
But I can promise you ...
That come what may,

Until the stars fall from the heavens above,
The horizon melts away and time ceases to be,
That you'll never have to face the world alone.

May I always be the light that leads you home,
The smile that greets you at day's end,
My embrace holding you tightly,
Your safe place from all else.

I'll be your unending love, evermore,
Yours forever, faithfully.
As you fall asleep every night,
Know this to be true,
For now and always,
How very much I love you.

Highest Walls, Deepest Love

She's been hurt so many times before, but still, she won't give up on love.
Not because she's foolish, but because she will never stop believing.
She's strong because she's never had any other options, and she loves with all her heart, because that's just who she is.
She doesn't do anything halfway and doesn't know how to turn off her feelings.
She's a wild heart on fire for living, and she fell in love with being alive a long time ago.
Her broken heart seems to always mend but her walls stay high.
She knows she must protect herself, but realizes that she's a lover and not meant to be alone.
Trying to be careful has never quite worked out for her,
Despite all the times she tried to not fall in love.
Her friends watch out for her because they care about her, probably more than she cares about herself.
She has a close circle and a huge heart and will do almost anything for anyone ...

Except herself, it seems.

She doesn't want to suffer another broken heart nor spend another night crying for love lost, but she ends up in that place, time and again.

She makes no apologies for the way she cares or who she chooses, and she embraces love with open arms, always.

She'd thought about changing her ways and sparing herself the pain, but she could never live that way.

She'd rather be burned alive in the flames of passion than to waste away in a life without love.

That would always be her choice and her way, and nothing could ever take that away from her ... But at least she knew who she was and what she wanted ...

She was born wild and lived her life aflame – heart, mind and soul.

Some would call her crazy or too intense, but she would never settle when it came to matters of her heart.

One thing was certain:

She was always willing to burn for those she loved.

Listen to Your Heart, but Take Your Head with You

I'm tired of making the safe choices.
I want to follow my heart and chase the stars.
Forget the ordinary love and mediocre passion,
I want to set the night on fire.
Everyone tells me to be reasonable and think everything through, but I've done that all my life.
I don't want to live by everyone else's rules, and I'm done playing it safe.
I want a love affair that makes my soul sigh with contentment.
I want the kisses that curl my toes and fill me with butterflies.
I want the one person who will make me dream of tomorrow in a way I've never known.
I don't want a lover, a love interest or someone to date,
I want my soulmate.
I need that person who sees my soul for its truth, accepts me for who I am and loves me unconditionally.
They'll tell me that I'm going to get my heart broken and I'm never going to be happy.

But I don't care what they say.
I want out of the labels and the boxes they try to put me in.
I want a wildfire love that sets my heart and soul on fire.
I deserve the kind of love that is once in a lifetime –
Respectful, fulfilling and passionate.
I know my worth, and I won't settle for anything less.
So, if you're going to come knocking on the walls to my heart, be prepared to bring your best self.
No judgment, expectations or jealousy.
An open and honest love that is compassionate and understanding.
I'm choosing today to listen to my heart, but I'll always take my head with me.
If you want to find me, you'll see me living my dreams and chasing the wind with a zealous courage that won't be defeated, diminished or destroyed.
So, if you're willing to live passionately, love faithfully and laugh with me endlessly,
Then let's go find some adventure ...
Me, you and forever.

Sometimes the Strongest Women Love beyond Faults, Cry behind Closed Doors and Fight Battles in Secret

She's the strongest person everyone knows,
A beautiful soul who seems to always be smiling and laughing ... But they only know what she wants them to know, they only see what she wants them to see.
She accepts and loves people for who they are, without judgement or expectation.
Her battles are the quiet ones no one knows about, behind closed doors and silent tears.
She cries from inexplicable sadness, momentary angst and absolute weariness.
Not the sort of tired that sleep can satisfy, but the deeper kind – a soulful fatigue that needs much more than rest.
She seeks no pity from those in her life, for she is the strong one ... Because sometimes, being strong is her only choice.
She loves with all her heart, lives every day to its fullest and gives everything her all.
She's learned to temper her expectations and depend on herself.
Strong-willed, sassy and feisty, she's the

woman that people never forget … and she makes sure her voice is heard.

Not just to talk, but because her words have meaning and her thoughts matter.

She's not a candle in the wind, she's a roaring wildfire.

It doesn't mean she doesn't fight internal battles of insecurities, fears and worry, only that she knows her strength and never gives up. She's not a fighter because she always wins, but because she never stays down.

She's okay with being a beautiful mess and a wonderful disaster,

Because she's not defined by all the things others focus on – flaws and imperfections.

She knows who she is and what she wants, and she won't stop until she's happy.

She's the strongest of women, but not in the way that people think –

She's tough in heart and hardy of soul.

She loves when she shouldn't, more than they may ever love her back ...

And yet, she still keeps pouring out her heart.

That's the beauty and blessing of a strong and soulful woman.

But What If We Find the Courage to Love Again?

I know it's been hard between us lately,
And we've had moments when we've lost our
way.
The magic that once sparked our love has
dissipated and the butterflies haven't been
around like they used to be.
It hurts my heart when we fight, and the tears I
cry crush my soul every time.
I don't know how we grew apart or why we
have such conflict at times, but I still believe –
In love ... In us ... In our future.
There have been many times when we wanted
to quit, that we didn't think we would make it.
They say that love alone isn't enough, but we
have more than that ... much more.
Respect, appreciation and passion … and the
strength to stand up for what we believe in.
Too often it seems we think with our hearts and
forget our heads.
We let hurt feelings and miscommunication
ruin the beautiful relationship we have …
But we can work together to fix that.
I don't know what tomorrow will bring, but I'm

not giving up on us ...
I hope you'll stand beside me and work through
it all, that you'll fight for us.
We have too much love and hope to quit on the
best thing that has ever happened to us.
I love you with all my heart and I always will –
That may not solve our problems, but it's a
start.
With great love and great hope we can find our
way, together.
It won't be easy and it won't be painless, but
with love in our hearts and passion in our
souls,
We can find the butterflies again ...
That's the happily ever after that I'm willing to
fight for,
The happiness I'm committed to working
towards.
Take my hand, hold my heart and let's start
believing in the love we've always had.
Let's remember the passion we've forgotten
along the way and start to believe in us again.
Together, we can make it through anything.
You, me and forever.
Let's find the courage to love each other again.

Sometimes the Wrong Choices Lead Us to the Right Places

I always thought I had it all figured out, knew where I was going and how to get there.
That's just when life seemed to change everything and turn it all upside down.
Somehow, I made all the wrong choices and ended up everywhere I never meant to be.
Tears of frustration clouded my vision, and all I could see is how much I wanted the things that were actually never meant for me.
The wrong loves, bad friends and poor decisions pushed me down the wrong roads ...
Or so I thought.
When I stopped asking for an easier path and started asking for more strength, things began to make sense.
Broken hearts weren't punishments, they were lessons.
Betrayed trust wasn't my fault, it was my warning.
Doors that closed to me were never meant to be opened.
I realized that life isn't a straight line, it's a circle – every end is a new beginning.

I know now what I never saw before – there's beauty in the moments and the little things aren't little at all ...

They're actually the big things.

The warm embrace of a missed friend, sweet kisses in the rain and the magical sunrise of a new day.

I'd never go back and change anything about where I've been, because it led me to exactly where I'm meant to be.

I truly believe that there are no coincidences and accidents aren't that at all ...

It's up to me to see the magic of the possibilities and find the doors to new opportunities.

With fire in my heart and passion in my spirit, I can do anything.

So, I'm keeping my face to the sunlight and the wind at my back.

Life is too amazing to not truly live it to the fullest.

Those places that I thought were wrong?

Turns out they were the right destinations after all.

They helped me understand what I never would have found otherwise ...

Most of all,

They showed me how to fall in love with being
alive ... every day.

With a full heart and a content soul, I'll always
love who I am and where I'm headed ...

It's a new day and I'm blessed ...

There's nothing I can't do.

Thank You for Reminding Me What Butterflies Feel Like

There once was a time when butterflies
Were a dream I had never known.
I'd spent my days chasing the wrong ones,
Never letting the right one catch me.

When you start listening to your heart
And stop hearing everyone else,
You begin to give yourself a chance
To find real and lasting love.

They say that love shows up
When you least expect it,
And I never could have foreseen you
And how you changed my life forever.

The way you love me at my worst,
And celebrate me at my best.
Holding my hand through the storms,
Dancing with me in the rain.

I never knew I was lost until you found me,
Never realized I was incomplete
Until you made me whole.

Two hearts, one beat and a beautiful future.

Nights spent lost in your arms,
Days wrapped up in your heart,
Most of all, thank you for always reminding me
What butterflies feel like with your kiss.

May You Spread Your Wings and Fly Free

As you wake up today, never forget how beautiful you are and how very much you are loved.

My wish for you is to find the hope in every day, the joy in the moments and the beauty all around you.

May you keep your face to the sunlight and see the wonder of a star-filled sky.

Know that while life may get you down sometimes, I'll always be by your side, holding your hand through the hard days and dancing with you in the good times.

My wish for you is to always soak in the beauty of nature and find the happiness in the faces of the people you see.

May you always chase your dreams, achieve the impossible and know that tomorrow, anything is possible.

If you're ever down, find me and I'll sing you the song of your heart, reminding you of the forgotten words.

Revel in the laughter of small children, the glee of small puppy kisses and the warm kindness of strangers you meet.

Always remember that you're special, one of a kind and made more beautiful by every one of your imperfections and scars.

Afterall, it's those lovely scars that tell your story.

May your worries stay small and your dreams stay big.

But most of all, my wish for you is to know that every day is a miracle, and that you are loved, beautiful and wonderful in all the ways that matter most.

So, enjoy the sunsets of your days with wistful smiles and sunrises with bright hopes for the day ...

For you can do anything if you truly believe in you ...

Like I always have and always will.

Today's your chance to start living the life you've always imagined ...

And I'll be right beside you, cheering you on.

CPSIA information can be obtained
at www.ICGtesting.com
Printed in the USA
LVHW101940160223
739692LV00018B/144